LUKE DIXON

Luke Dixon is a director, teacher and academic. He is internationally known for both productions of Shakespeare and site-specific work. He has directed and led workshops on Shakespeare around the world, from *A Midsummer Night's Dream* in Brazil to *Macbeth* in Hong Kong via *Pericles* in South Africa.

Luke is also editor of *Shakespeare Monologues for Men*, *Women* and *Young Men* in this series, and author of *Play-Acting: A Guide to Theatre Workshops*. For more information, see www.lukedixon.co.uk

D0833099

THE GOOD AUDITION GUIDES

CLASSICAL MONOLOGUES
edited by Marina Caldarone

SHAKESPEARE MONOLOGUES
edited by Luke Dixon

SHAKESPEARE MONOLOGUES FOR YOUNG PEOPLE
edited by Luke Dixon

MODERN MONOLOGUES
edited by Trilby James

The Good Audition Guides

SHAKESPEARE MONOLOGUES FOR YOUNG WOMEN

edited and introduced by

LUKE DIXON

NICK HERN BOOKS
London
www.nickhernbooks.co.uk

A NICK HERN BOOK

The Good Audition Guides:
Shakespeare Monologues for Young Women
first published in Great Britain in 2012
by Nick Hern Books Limited
The Glasshouse, 49a Goldhawk Road, London W12 8QP

Introduction copyright © 2012 Luke Dixon
Copyright in this selection © 2012 Nick Hern Books Ltd

Cover design: www.energydesignstudio.com

Typeset by Nick Hern Books, London
Printed and bound by CPI Group (UK) Ltd

A CIP catalogue record for this book
is available from the British Library

ISBN 978 1 84842 266 7

MIX
Paper from
responsible sources
FSC
www.fsc.org   FSC® C013604

Contents

Introduction

WHY SHAKESPEARE? ☞

The basic requirements for most auditions, from drama-school entry to a season with the Royal Shakespeare Company, will include a speech by Shakespeare. Faced with the thirty-eight plays that are generally considered to have been written by Shakespeare, it is daunting for even the most experienced actor to know where to begin in finding a suitable speech.

The Shakespearean canon, that is all the plays he wrote which have survived, are the heart of English drama. A speech from one of those plays can provide an actor with opportunities to show off their skills and talent in a whole range of ways: vocally and physically, in terms of characterisation and storytelling, emotionally and intellectually. A Shakespeare speech is the best tool for an actor to demonstrate their craft and for an audition panel or director to appreciate and judge it.

SHAKESPEARE AND HIS STAGE ☞

William Shakespeare was born in 1564 in Stratford-upon-Avon and went to the local school. He married Anne Hathaway in 1582. William was eighteen, Anne twenty-six. Their daughter Susanna was born the following year, and twins Hamnet and Judith in 1585. What happened next remains a mystery but eight years later Shakespeare was working successfully in the theatre in London and by the age of thirty was co-owner, actor and main playwright for London's leading theatre company, the Lord Chamberlain's Men. After James I came to the throne in 1603 they became known as the King's Men. The company built their own theatre on the south bank of the Thames and called it The Globe. A modern replica stands near the site of the original.

It was for that theatre that Shakespeare wrote his best-known plays. They were written to be acted on a stage thrust out into a large crowd standing all around and with banks of seats high up to an open sky. Performing in daylight with little scenery and no lighting, the actors had to create place, time and atmosphere with just their own acting skills and the words given to them by Shakespeare. An actor in the audition room today faces the same challenges, to turn a bare space into a Greek palace (Helena, *A Midsummer Night's Dream*), a shepherd's cottage (Perdita, *The Winter's Tale*), the Forest of Arden (*As You Like It*), a field of battle (Joan la Pucelle, *Henry VI, Part One*) or a brothel (Marina, *Pericles*).

Thirty-six of Shakespeare's plays were collected after his death by his colleagues and printed in what is known as the First Folio, a folio being the size of the sheet of paper it was printed on. A thousand copies were printed and they sold for £1 each. About 230 still exist and now sell for around £3 million each. A couple of other plays only appeared in what are known as quarto editions, on paper folded to half the size of a folio sheet. For publication, each of the plays was divided into five parts, known as acts. The first act was the introduction or exposition, the second a development of the action, the third a climax or crisis, the fourth more development, and the fifth a resolution. The acts are usually divided into a number of smaller parts called scenes.

THE SPEECHES IN THIS BOOK ☞

This is one of two books of Shakespeare speeches for young people: one for young men and one for young women. There are two companion volumes of speeches for older actors. All the speeches were first spoken by boys and young men – there were no female actors in Shakespeare's day – so it can sometimes be interesting to consider boys' speeches if you are a girl, and girls' speeches if you are a boy. Some characters (citizens, for example, or supernatural creatures) can be thought of as gender neutral, that is appropriate to be played by either men or women. Some of these characters (though with different speeches) can be found in both this volume and the companion volume of speeches for young men.

The speeches vary greatly in length. There are some very short pieces for those who find the task of learning lines difficult. In some cases there are short speeches which can easily be joined together by the more adventurous young actor to create something more substantial.

CHOOSING YOUR SPEECH ☞

In this volume I have brought together forty speeches, from amongst the best known to the least common. You will never find a 'new' Shakespeare speech. Fashion and contemporary performance are often factors in which speeches are currently popular and you can never second-guess what speech the actor before or after you will perform. Best to find a speech that you like, enjoy performing, and can in some way empathise with. Do not worry about what other actors might be doing.

Choose more than one speech to have in your repertoire so that you always have something suitable when the call comes. Having chosen a speech, read the play, and find the backstory so you know where the character and the speech are coming from.

Once you have found a speech that you like and that you think suits you, get hold of a copy of the complete play so that you can work on the speech in context. If that seems daunting, find a film of the play to watch first. There are innumerable editions of the plays of Shakespeare. Those editing them often disagree about the numbering of the scenes and lines. So do not be surprised if the copy of the play that you are using does not agree exactly with the act, scene, and line numbers given in this book.

Complexity Some of the speeches in this book are relatively simple and might be more useful for the actor for whom Shakespeare is a new and terrifying experience. Miranda in *The Tempest* and Juliet in *Romeo and Juliet* perhaps fall into this category. Others, such as Ophelia in *Hamlet* and Helena in *All's Well That Ends Well*, are rich and complex in the language, thought or emotion and might be more suitable for actors seeking a challenge or needing to show the full range of their abilities.

Age It is rare that we know the age of a character in a play by Shakespeare. In a production the director will have made decisions about the age of his characters and their relative ages to each other. In an audition you can be much more flexible in deciding whether the speech of a character is suited to you and your playing age.

Gender None of these speeches were written to be acted by a woman. Actresses did not exist in Shakespeare's London and all the plays were written to be acted by men and boys. Gender and the dissemblance of gender is an important theme through many of the plays. There are speeches here, both comic and serious, which give you plenty of opportunity to play with gender, from Joan la Pucelle in *King Henry VI, Part One* to Rosalind in *As You Like It*.

Length The speeches vary considerably in the number of their words but not necessarily in the time they take to perform. Miranda's speech in *The Tempest* is quite short in the number of words, but contains a good deal of implied action as she offers to help Ferdinand pile his logs. Joan la Pucelle's speech in *Henry VI, Part One*, where she conjures spirits, has plenty of words but also a great amount of implied action, noise and silence. It is a speech that needs to be given space to breathe and for the spaces, sounds and silences within it to be found. In these and many other speeches there are important moments when the character is listening or when she is waiting for or expecting a reply (Rosalind in *As You Like It* and Juliet in *Romeo and Juliet*). These moments between the words can make a speech come fully alive. Where some speeches are too long for audition purposes I have, as judiciously as possible, made cuts.

LANGUAGE ☞

Shakespeare's audiences went to 'hear' plays. It was not until long after his death that anyone wrote of going to 'see' a play. So the sounds of Shakespeare's words are as important as their meanings. Indeed the sounds often help convey the meanings. Enjoy and play with the sounds as you work through the speeches.

Prose is everyday speech but Shakespeare often heightens that speech, giving it colour, richness, images and so on that we would not use in our everyday lives.

Poetry is where that heightened use of language is taken further and the speech goes beyond the everyday and rhythm becomes important.

Verse is poetry where the rhythms of the words are organised.

Iambic pentameter is a particular kind of verse. An 'iamb' is where a short syllable is followed by a long syllable giving a 'di-dum' rhythm. 'Metre' is how rhythms are organised in lines of verse. 'Penta' is the old Greek word for five. So if you put five iambs in a line of verse you get an iambic pentameter:

> *di-dum, di-dum, di-dum, di-dum, di-dum*

This was the main form Shakespeare used in writing his plays: it is the heartbeat of his language. Sometimes it is used rigidly and is easy to spot:

> *Thou know'st the mask of night is on my face;*
> *Else would a maiden blush bepaint my cheek*

> (Juliet, *Romeo and Juliet*)

Sometimes, especially as he got older and more experienced, he played with the form and pulled it around for emotional, dramatic or characterisation effect.

In order for the rhythm to work a word ending in '-*ed*' will sometimes have the letters stressed as a syllable (in which case it is printed '-*èd*'), and sometimes it will not be a separate syllable but be spoken as if the 'e' is not there (in which case it is printed '-'*d*').

Rhyming couplets Sometimes Shakespeare uses rhyme and when two lines together rhyme we have a rhyming couplet. Often these are used at the end of a speech or scene to indicate finality.

Punctuation in Shakespeare is a controversial subject. Shakespeare did not prepare his plays for publication and therefore the punctuation in the texts is largely put there by his colleagues or the publisher or printer. Nonetheless, the punctuation in these speeches, following for the most part the First Folio, can give you some help not just with sense but also with where to breathe, pause, rest, change gear, or change thought.

Vocabulary Shakespeare wrote at a time when English as we know it was developing rapidly. He made up, or used very early in the development of the English langauge, many words and phrases that have become part of our everyday speech. Words that we find first in Shakespeare include accommodation, critic, dwindle, eventful, exposure, frugal, generous, gloomy, laughable, majestic, misplaced, monumental, multitudinous and obscene. Phrases that he coined include disgraceful conduct, elbow room, fair play, green-eyed monster, clothes make the man, method in his madness, to thine own self be true, the lady doth protest too much, and it's Greek to me. Sometimes he used a word which was never used again. Some of the words he used which are familiar today had different or stronger meanings then than now and these I have glossed in the notes.

THE AUDITION ☞

Thought process It is rare that a character in Shakespeare sets out to make a speech, though in some of the big public and political scenes a character does just that. Joan la Pucelle in *Henry VI, Part One* publicly curses her English captors as she is about to be executed; Desdemona in *Othello* has come prepared to defend herself before her father and the Duke.

But for the most part a speech does start with a single thought which is followed by another and then another until a speech has been said. So allow time for each of those thoughts to come and be fresh in the mind before they are spoken. Do not be daunted by what can seem endless lines of text. It is not a race to get through to the end. Take the speech one thought at a time.

Structure   As you follow the thoughts, follow too the emotions and language of the speech. Look for its structure. Allow yourself to show the full range of emotion and vocal possibility within the speech. Seek variety. None of these speeches is on one note. All allow a wide range of vocal and emotional expression.

Setting and geography   Many of these speeches are soliloquies allowing the character to express her thoughts or ideas to an audience while she is alone, such as Juliet in *Romeo and Juliet*. Other speeches, like Desdemona's in *Othello*, are parts of dialogues or conversations. And some, such as the First Citizen's in *King John*, are directed to large public gatherings. Others may be a combination of all these. Decide who else, if anyone, is there to hear the speech and where they are placed. Give thought to the geography or layout of the place the speech is being spoken in – be they the woods of *A Midsummer Night's Dream*, Elsinore Castle in *Hamlet*, or the windswept island of *The Tempest*. Take a few moments when you first come into the audition room to place the other characters and recreate the geography and setting in your mind's eye.

Audience   If your speech is directed to an audience, that can be a theatre audience or an audience within the scene. Some speeches are soliloquies which can be played to oneself, to the audience, or some combination of the two (Helena in *All's Well That Ends Well*). Others are to a public audience within the play (Desdemona in *Othello*). Decide whether and how to use your audition panel as that audience.

Make the space your own   Many other actors will have been in the audition room before you. Many will come after you.

Spend a moment or two before you start your speech focusing and allowing the panel to focus on you. Create the silence out of which your words will come and decide on the energy that the words will bring with them, whether the distress and anguish of The Jailer's Daughter in *The Two Noble Kinsmen* alone at night watching a ship being wrecked at sea, or Juliet in *Romeo and Juliet* alone in her bedroom willing her new husband to arrive.

HOW TO USE THIS BOOK

For each speech, as well as specifying who is speaking, I have given an indication of:

WHERE ☞ If possible I have indicated where and when the action is taking place. Sometimes this can be very specific, either because Shakespeare has told us or because the action is tied to a particular historical event. Often the plays are set in times of legend or myth and the date and place are of no direct importance in affecting how you perform them.

WHO ELSE IS THERE ☞ This note gives an indication of who else is on stage and the character's relationship to them.

WHAT IS HAPPENING ☞ This note will give a context for the speech, but it is not a substitute for reading the play and yourself deciding where the speech is coming from.

WHAT TO THINK ABOUT ☞ I have indicated some ideas of things to think about as you are working on the speech. This is by no means an exhaustive list, but will give you a way into the speech and should spark other thoughts and ideas of your own.

WHERE ELSE TO LOOK ☞ If you like a speech or character and want to look elsewhere for similar pieces this note will help you on your way.

GLOSSARY ☞ I have glossed the trickier and perplexing words, phrases and thoughts in the speeches, but do not worry if you need a dictionary or annotated edition of the play to help you fully understand what your character is saying.

THE TEXTS ☞ Wherever possible I have used the exemplary texts of The Shakespeare Folios published by Nick Hern Books and edited by Nick de Somogyi (to whom my thanks for his excellent help and advice in editing this volume). Speeches from plays not yet published in this series have been edited by me from the First Folio using the same editorial rules. In the case of *Pericles* and *The Two Noble Kinsmen*, neither of which appears in the First Folio and both of which are of contested authorship, I have used quarto texts edited in the same way. All the glosses are my own.

The following categories may help you find a particular attribute that suits you, or your audition needs:

- HIGH STATUS

    The Princess in *Love's Labour's Lost*
    Anne Boleyn in *Henry VIII*
    Desdemona in *Othello*
    Cordelia in *King Lear*
    Imogen in *Cymbeline*

- LOW STATUS

    A Courtesan in *The Comedy of Errors*
    Mistress Quickly in *Henry IV, Part Two*
    The Jailer's Daughter in *The Two Noble Kinsmen*

- DAUGHTERS AND SISTERS

    Miranda in *The Tempest*
    Portia in *The Merchant of Venice*
    Ophelia in *Hamlet*
    Cordelia in *King Lear*
    The Jailer's Daughter in *The Two Noble Kinsmen*

- IN LOVE

    Miranda in *The Tempest*
    Julia in *The Two Gentlemen of Verona*
    Helena in *A Midsummer Night's Dream*
    Portia in *The Merchant of Venice*

Helena in *All's Well That Ends Well*
Cressida in *Troilus and Cressida*
Juliet in *Romeo and Juliet*
The Jailer's Daughter in *The Two Noble Kinsmen*

- SCARY

  Joan la Pucelle in *Henry VI, Part One*
  Hecate in *Macbeth*

- COMIC

  A Courtesan in *The Comedy of Errors*
  Hero in *Much Ado About Nothing*
  Mistress Quickly in *Henry IV, Part Two*

- ANXIOUS

  Anne Boleyn in *Henry VIII*
  Imogen in *Cymbeline*

- ANGRY

  Adriana in *The Comedy of Errors*
  A Courtesan in *The Comedy of Errors*
  Hermia in *A Midsummer Night's Dream*
  Marina in *Pericles*
  Mistress Quickly *in Henry IV, Part Two*
  Joan la Pucelle in *Henry VI, Part One*
  Desdemona in *Othello*

- SAD

  Ophelia in *Hamlet*
  Cordelia in *King Lear*

- SUPERNATURAL

  Ariel in *The Tempest*
  Puck in *A Midsummer Night's Dream*
  Hecate in *Macbeth*

The Comedies

The Tempest

WHO ☞ *Miranda.*

WHERE ☞ *A remote island.*

WHO ELSE IS THERE ☞ *Ferdinand, son of the Duke of Naples.*

WHAT IS HAPPENING ☞ *As a small child Miranda was shipwrecked on the island with her father Prospero. Many years later Ferdinand is also shipwrecked on the island and has become separated from his companions. Prospero has imprisoned Ferdinand and given him hard tasks to do. Miranda, having never before seen any human being except her father, has fallen in love with Ferdinand. As he piles up thousands of logs on Prospero's orders, Miranda tells him not to work so hard and offers to help him.*

WHAT TO THINK ABOUT ☞

- *Where is Ferdinand and where are the logs he is moving?*

- *How close is Prospero and how careful must Miranda be not to disturb him?*

- *What must it be like to be a teenage girl and see another human for the first time?*

WHERE ELSE TO LOOK ☞ *Talking to the men they love are Portia (The Merchant of Venice, pp. 42 and 44) and Cressida (Troilus and Cressida, p. 76).*

Miranda

" Alas, now, pray you,
Work not so hard! I would the lightning had
Burnt up those logs that you are enjoin'd* to pile!
Pray, set it down and rest you: when this* burns,
'Twill weep for having wearied you. My father
Is hard at study; pray now, rest yourself;
He's safe for these three hours.
                         If you'll sit down,
I'll bear* your logs the while: pray, give me that;
I'll carry it to the pile.
                  It would become me
As well as it does you; and I should do it
With much more ease, for my good will is to it,
And yours it is against. **"**

(*Act 3, scene 1, lines 15–31, with cuts*)

GLOSSARY

enjoin'd – forced
this – i.e. this wood
bear – carry

The Tempest

WHO ☞   *Ariel, an airy spirit.*

WHERE ☞   *A remote island.*

WHO ELSE IS THERE ☞   *Alonso, King of Naples, Sebastian (his brother) and Antonio (Prospero's brother), together with other members of Alonso's court. Antonio is the cause of Prospero's banishment to the island many years before.*

WHAT IS HAPPENING ☞   *Alonso, Sebastian, Antonio and the others have recently been shipwrecked by Ariel at Prospero's command. Ariel appears to them as a harpy (half human, half bird), to scare them, and they draw their swords to defend themselves.*

WHAT TO THINK ABOUT ☞

- *How scary can you be? And how can you create a monstrous creature with your body, voice and movements?*

- *Ariel has other spirits with him. Decide where they are, and where the men being talked to are positioned.*

- *Be clear in telling each of the men what they have done wrong.*

WHERE ELSE TO LOOK ☞   *Puck (A Midsummer Night's Dream, p. 40) also scares his audience.*

Ariel

" You fools! I and my fellows
Are ministers of Fate. The elements
Of whom your swords are temper'd may as well
Wound the loud winds, or with bemock'd-at stabs
Kill the still-closing waters, as diminish
One dowle that's in my plume.* My fellow ministers
Are like invulnerable. If you could hurt,
Your swords are now too massy* for your strengths,
And will not be uplifted. But remember —
For that's my business to you – that you three
From Milan did supplant good Prospero;*
Expos'd unto the sea, which hath requit it,
Him and his innocent child; for which foul deed,
The powers, delaying, not forgetting, have
Incens'd the seas and shores, yea, all the creatures,
Against your peace. Thee of thy son, Alonso,
They have bereft; and do pronounce by me
Lingering perdition,* worse than any death
Can be at once, shall step by step attend
You and your ways; whose wraths to guard you from –
Which here in this most desolate isle else falls
Upon your heads – is nothing but heart's sorrow
And a clear life ensuing. **"**

(Act 3, scene 3, lines 59–81)

GLOSSARY

may as well… plume – you might as well try to injure the wind or kill the
    seas as damage a single feather in my plumage
massy – heavy
From Milan did supplant… Prospero – banished Prospero from Milan
    (pronounced to rhyme with 'villain')
Lingering perdition – enduring punishment

The Two Gentlemen of Verona

WHO ☞ *Julia.*

WHERE ☞ *A room in Julia's house in Verona, Italy.*

WHO ELSE IS THERE ☞ *Her waiting-woman Lucetta.*

WHAT IS HAPPENING ☞ *Julia is in love with Proteus. She is planning to travel to Milan to visit him. Since that journey would be arduous, Lucetta suggests she waits for Proteus's return, and temper the force of her passion, but Julia brushes her objections aside.*

WHAT TO THINK ABOUT ☞

- *What is it about Proteus that Julia loves so much and how is she so certain of his love for her?*

- *What is the age and status of Lucetta and how does this affect the way in which Julia talks to her?*

- *What experiences, if any, has Julia had to make her so certain in her opinions?*

WHERE ELSE TO LOOK ☞ *Portia (The Merchant of Venice, pp. 42 and 44), Juliet (Romeo and Juliet, p. 84) and Desdemona (Othello, pp. 92 and 94) are also made bold by their belief in the power of love.*

Julia

" O, know'st thou not his looks are my soul's food?
Pity the dearth that I have pinèd in*
By longing for that food so long a time.
Didst thou but know the inly* touch of love,
Thou wouldst as soon go kindle fire with snow
As seek to quench the fire of love with words.
The more thou damm'st it up, the more it burns.
The current that with gentle murmur glides,
Thou know'st, being stopp'd, impatiently doth rage;
But when his fair course is not hinderèd,
He makes sweet music with th' enamell'd* stones,
Giving a gentle kiss to every sedge*
He overtaketh in his pilgrimage,
And so by many winding nooks he strays
With willing sport to the wild ocean.
Then let me go* and hinder not my course,
I'll be as patient as a gentle stream
And make a pastime of each weary step
Till the last step have brought me to my love;
And there I'll rest, as after much turmoil
A blessèd soul doth in Elysium.* **"**

(Act 2, scene 7, lines 15–38, with cut)

GLOSSARY

Pity the dearth that I have pinèd in – feel sorry for the lack (i.e. of love)
    that I have starved for
inly – internal
enamell'd – brightly coloured, sparkling
sedge – reed
Then let me go – so if you allow me to go
Elysium – heaven

The Comedy of Errors

WHO ☞ *Adriana, wife to Antipholus of Ephesus.*

WHERE ☞ *The market place in Ephesus.*

WHO ELSE IS THERE ☞ *Her sister Luciana, Antipholus of Syracuse, and his servant Dromio of Syracuse.*

WHAT IS HAPPENING ☞ *Identical twins (both called Antipholus) are separated at birth, and each has a servant called Dromio, also identical twins. The arrival of Antipholus of Syracuse and his servant in Ephesus, home town of his brother, causes the confusion of the play. Adriana has just run into Antipholus of Syracuse at the market. She assumes him to be her husband and is angry when he does not acknowledge her. She accuses him of being unfaithful.*

WHAT TO THINK ABOUT ☞

- *How much does Adriana love and trust her husband?*
- *Does she really believe he is unfaithful, and if so why?*
- *Antipholus does not respond. Does Adriana give him any opportunity to reply or does she just keep talking?*

WHERE ELSE TO LOOK ☞ *Angry and confused at the behaviour of their loved ones are Helena (A Midsummer Night's Dream, p. 34) and Hermia (A Midsummer Night's Dream, p. 38).*

Adriana

❝ Ay, ay, Antipholus, look strange and frown;
Some other mistress hath thy sweet aspects.
I am not Adriana nor thy wife.
The time was once when thou unurg'd* wouldst vow
That never words were music to thine ear,
That never object pleasing in thine eye,
That never touch well welcome to thy hand,
That never meat sweet-savour'd* in thy taste,
Unless I spake, or look'd, or touch'd, or carv'd to thee.

How comes it now, my husband, O, how comes it,
That thou art then estrangèd from thyself?
Thyself I call it, being strange to me,
That, undividable, incorporate,
Am better than thy dear self's better part.*
Ah, do not tear away thyself from me!
For know, my love, as easy mayst thou fall
A drop of water in the breaking gulf,
And take unmingled that same drop again,
Without addition or diminishing,
As take from me thyself and not me too.*
How dearly would it touch thee to the quick*
Shouldst thou but hear I were licentious,*
And that this body, consecrate to thee,
By ruffian* lust should be contaminate!
Wouldst thou not spit at me, and spurn at me,
And hurl the name of husband in my face,
And tear the stain'd skin off my harlot brow,*
And from my false hand cut the wedding-ring,
And break it with a deep-divorcing vow?
I know thou canst; and therefore see thou do it.
I am possess'd with an adulterate blot:*
My blood is mingled with the crime of lust;
For if we too be one, and thou play false,
I do digest the poison of thy flesh,
Being strumpeted* by thy contagion.
Keep then fair league* and truce with thy true bed,
I live unstain'd, thou undishonourèd. **99**

(Act 2, scene 2, lines 114–50)

GLOSSARY

unurg'd – unprompted, without urging   *sweet-savour'd* – delicious
better part – higher qualities
as easy… and not me too – you can as easily spill a drop of water into the
    sea and take it out again as seek to separate from me
quick – heart, core   *licentious* – lustful
ruffian – brutal, violent   *my harlot brow* – my adulterous face
blot – disgraceful stain   *strumpeted* – made into a prostitute
Keep then fair league – if you observe the true contract

The Comedy of Errors

WHO ☞ *A Courtesan.*

WHERE ☞ *The marketplace in Ephesus.*

WHO ELSE IS THERE ☞ *Antipholus of Syracuse and his servant Dromio of Syracuse.*

WHAT IS HAPPENING ☞ *The story of The Comedy of Errors is of identical twins separated at birth. Both are called Antipholus and each has a servant called Dromio, both of whom are identical twins. The arrival of Antipholus of Syracuse and his servant in Ephesus, home town of his brother, causes the confusion of the play. The Courtesan has given Antipholus of Ephesus an expensive ring in exchange for a 'chain' (or necklace). Meeting Antipholus of Syracuse at the market, and mistaking him for his brother, she asks him for the chain he owes her. Antipholus and Dromio go off accusing her of being a witch.*

WHAT TO THINK ABOUT ☞

- *Is the Courtesan talking to the audience or just to herself?*

- *How important is the money to her? Is forty ducats a lot?*

- *Does her mood change during the speech and, if so, how?*

WHERE ELSE TO LOOK ☞ *Adriana (The Comedy of Errors, p. 26) is also confused by the two Antipholuses, thinking the brother to be her husband.*

A Courtesan

66 Now, out of doubt* Antipholus is mad,
Else would he never so demean himself.
A ring he hath of mine worth forty ducats,
And for the same he promis'd me a chain:
Both one and other he denies me now.
The reason that I gather he is mad,
Besides this present instance of his rage,
Is a mad tale he told today at dinner,
Of his own doors being shut against his entrance.
Belike his wife, acquainted with his fits,*
On purpose shut the doors against his way.
My way is now to hie* home to his house,
And tell his wife that, being lunatic,
He rush'd into my house and took perforce*
My ring away. This course I fittest choose;*
For forty ducats is too much to lose. **99**

(Act 4, scene 3, lines 82–97)

GLOSSARY

out of doubt – certainly, beyond the shadow of a doubt
Belike… fits – presumably… moods
hie – hurry
perforce – by force
This course I fittest choose – I choose this to be the best course

Much Ado About Nothing

WHO ☞ *Hero.*

WHERE ☞ *The garden of Leonato, Hero's father.*

WHO ELSE IS THERE ☞ *Margaret and Ursula, Hero's waiting-gentlewomen. Beatrice is hiding in the background, eavesdropping on the scene.*

WHAT IS HAPPENING ☞ *Hero's cousin Beatrice will have nothing to do with men. Hero and her female servants are plotting to make Beatrice fall in love with the lofty and sarcastic Benedick by pretending that he is in love with her. Knowing that Beatrice is listening, Hero is accusing her of pride, stubbornness and contrariness when it comes to men.*

WHAT TO THINK ABOUT ☞

- *Where is everybody? Where are Margaret and Ursula, and where is Beatrice hiding?*

- *How much fun are the three having with this conspiracy?*

- *Might it be difficult to keep a straight face, and might it be hard to suppress the occasional giggle?*

- *How loudly and in what direction does Hero have to speak to ensure that Beatrice hears her?*

WHERE ELSE TO LOOK ☞ *Rosalind (As You Like It, p. 48) also interferes in the love affairs of others.*

Hero

❝ O god of love! I know he doth deserve
As much as may be yielded to* a man:
But Nature never fram'd a woman's heart
Of prouder stuff than that of Beatrice.
Disdain and scorn ride sparkling in her eyes,
Misprising* what they look on, and her wit
Values itself so highly that to her
All matter else seems weak: she cannot love,
Nor take no shape nor project of affection,*
She is so self-endear'd.*
                I never yet saw man,
How wise, how noble, young, how rarely featur'd,*
But she would spell him backward:* if fair-fac'd,
She would swear the gentleman should be her sister;
If black,* why, Nature, drawing of an antic,*
Made a foul blot; if tall, a lance ill-headed;*
If low, an agate very vilely cut;*
If speaking, why, a vane blown with all winds;
If silent, why, a block movèd with none.
So turns she every man the wrong side out
And never gives to truth and virtue that
Which simpleness and merit purchaseth. **❞**

(*Act 3, scene 1, lines 48–72, with cut*)

GLOSSARY

yielded to – granted of, credited to
Misprising – misconstruing (i.e. deliberately undervaluing)
take no shape nor project of affection – conceive neither the form or scope
    of love
self-endear'd – in love with herself
rarely featur'd – good looking
spell him backward – reverse his qualities
black – swarthy
antic – grotesque clown (the image is of a scratchily drawn and ugly
    caricature)
ill-headed – with a blunt or mis-shapen blade
If low, an agate very vilely cut – if short, a badly carved miniature cameo

Love's Labour's Lost

WHO ☞ *The Princess of France.*

WHERE ☞ *The King of Navarre's park.*

WHO ELSE IS THERE ☞ *Lord Boyet and others.*

WHAT IS HAPPENING ☞ *The Princess has come on behalf of her father, the King of France, to negotiate a settlement over who shall rule the province of Aquitaine. The proposal is that if France can rule Aquitaine, Navarre can have the hand of the Princess in marriage. But the King of Navarre has made a vow that he will allow no woman to enter his court for three years while he lives in silent study. Boyet tells the Princess that nature deprived the rest of the world by giving so much beauty to her. She replies that she does not need his praise.*

WHAT TO THINK ABOUT ☞

- *What hopes, personal and political, does the Princess have for these negotiations?*

- *What does she know of the King of Navarre? Is he an attractive potential husband?*

- *Note how clear and precise she is in her orders.*

WHERE ELSE TO LOOK ☞ *Aware of her own attractiveness, and similarly in command of the scene, is Rosalind (As You Like It, p. 48).*

Princess

" Good Lord Boyet, my beauty, though but mean,
Needs not the painted flourish of your praise:
Beauty is bought by judgement of the eye,
Not utter'd by base sale of chapmen's tongues.*
I am less proud to hear you tell my worth
Than you much willing to be counted wise
In spending your wit in the praise of mine.
But now to task the tasker: good Boyet,
You are not ignorant, all-telling fame
Doth noise abroad Navarre hath made a vow,
Till painful study shall outwear three years
No woman may approach his silent court.
Therefore to's* seemeth it a needful course,
Before we enter his forbidden gates,
To know his pleasure; and in that behalf,
Bold of your worthiness, we single you
As our best-moving fair solicitor.*
Tell him, the daughter of the King of France,
On serious business craving quick dispatch,
Importunes* personal conference with his grace.
Haste, signify so much; while we attend,
Like humble-visag'd suitors, his high will. **"**

(Act 2, scene 1, lines 15–36)

GLOSSARY

the base sale of chapmen's tongues – the tawdry sales-pitch of market
      traders
to's – to us
best-moving... solicitor – most persuasive... advocate
Importunes – (stressed on the second syllable) craves
humble-visag'd – i.e. wearing suitably humble expressions

A Midsummer Night's Dream

WHO ☞   *Helena, in love with Demetrius.*

WHERE ☞   *The Palace of Theseus, Duke of Athens.*

WHO ELSE IS THERE ☞   *Lysander and Hermia, in love with one another.*

WHAT IS HAPPENING ☞   *Helena is in love with Demetrius. But he is in love with her best friend Hermia, who is in love with Lysander. Helena has just met up with Hermia and Lysander, and Hermia has called her 'fair Helena'.*

WHAT TO THINK ABOUT ☞

- *What does Helena think Demetrius sees in Hermia but not in her?*

- *What does Helena see in Demetrius that makes her so in love with him?*

- *How is the friendship between Helena and Hermia disrupted by what is going on?*

- *The speech is written in rhyming couplets (pairs of rhyming lines). Find ways to use the rhymes to advance Helena's thoughts – but avoid letting them get in the way of the meaning of the sentences.*

WHERE ELSE TO LOOK ☞   *The tables are turned later in the play when it is Hermia whose love is unrequited (A Midsummer Night's Dream, p. 38), as is that of another Helena (All's Well That Ends Well, p. 50).*

Helena

❝ Call you me fair?* That 'fair' again unsay.
Demetrius loves your fair: O happy fair!
Your eyes are lode-stars,* and your tongue's sweet air
More tuneable* than lark to shepherd's ear
When wheat is green, when hawthorn buds appear.
Sickness is catching: O, were favour* so,
Yours would I catch, fair Hermia, ere I go;
My ear should catch your voice, my eye your eye,
My tongue should catch your tongue's sweet melody.
Were the world mine, Demetrius being bated,*
The rest I'd give to be to you translated.*
O, teach me how you look, and with what art
You sway the motion of Demetrius' heart. **❞**

(*Act 1, scene 1, lines 181–93*)

GLOSSARY

fair – beautiful
lode-stars – guiding stars
tuneable – harmonious
favour – attraction
bated – held back (i.e. if I owned the whole world except for Demetrius)
translated – transformed

A Midsummer Night's Dream

WHO ☞ *Puck (or Robin Goodfellow), a mischievous spirit.*

WHERE ☞ *A wood near Athens.*

WHO ELSE IS THERE ☞ *Oberon, King of the Fairies.*

WHAT IS HAPPENING ☞ *Oberon has asked Puck to help him achieve revenge against Titania, his wife, with whom he has quarrelled. He has ordered Puck to gather a magic flower and told her to put the juice from it on Titania's eyes while she is asleep: the magic properties of the flower will make her fall in love with the first thing that she sees on waking up. Puck tells Oberon how she came across a group of humble workmen ('rude mechanicals') rehearsing the play of 'Pyramus and Thisbe'. When one of the workmen left the stage, Puck transformed his head into a donkey's. The braying noise he made woke Titania – and she immediately fell in love with him.*

WHAT TO THINK ABOUT ☞

- *How does Puck dramatise all the different people in his story?*

- *Find ways for Puck to maintain the suspense as he tells his story to Oberon.*

- *Play with the ways in which Puck can move as a spirit creature.*

WHERE ELSE TO LOOK ☞ *Ariel is another supernatural creature reporting back to her master (The Tempest, p. 22).*

Puck

“ My mistress with a monster is in love.
Near to her close* and consecrated bower,
While she was in her dull and sleeping hour,
A crew of patches,* rude mechanicals,
That work for bread upon Athenian stalls,
Were met together to rehearse a play

Intended for great Theseus' nuptial day.*
The shallowest thick-skin of that barren sort,*
Who Pyramus presented in their sport,
Forsook his scene and enter'd in a brake,
When I did him at this advantage take:
An ass's nole* I fixèd on his head.
Anon his Thisbe must be answerèd,
And forth my mimic comes. When they him spy,
As wild geese that the creeping fowler eye,
Or russet-pated choughs,* many in sort,
Rising and cawing at the gun's report,
Sever themselves and madly sweep the sky,
So, at his sight, away his fellows fly;
And, at our stamp, here o'er and o'er one falls;
He 'Murder' cries and help from Athens calls.
Their sense thus weak, lost with their fears thus strong,
Made senseless things begin to do them wrong;
For briers and thorns at their apparel snatch;
Some sleeves, some hats, from yielders all things catch.
I led them on in this distracted fear,
And left sweet Pyramus translated there:
When in that moment, so it came to pass,
Titania waked and straightway loved an ass. 99

(*Act 3, scene 2, lines 6–34*)

GLOSSARY

close – secret
patches – fools
nuptial day – wedding day
shallowest thick-skin of that barren sort – stupidest dolt out of that witless
 company
ass's nole – donkey's head
choughs – jackdaws

A Midsummer Night's Dream

WHO ☞   *Hermia, in love with Lysander.*

WHERE ☞   *The woods outside Athens.*

WHO ELSE IS THERE ☞   *Demetrius.*

WHAT IS HAPPENING ☞   *Hermia and Lysander are in love and have run away together. Lost in the woods, they find somewhere to sleep for the night. Demetrius is also unrequitedly in love with Hermia. When Hermia wakes up she finds that Lysander has disappeared and that Demetrius is there in his place. She suspects Demetrius of having killed Lysander while he slept.*

WHAT TO THINK ABOUT ☞

- *Does Hermia really believe that Demetrius has killed Lysander or is she being dramatic?*

- *How frightening is it to be lost in the woods, sleep rough, and wake to find your boyfriend has disappeared?*

- *The speech is written in rhyming couplets (pairs of rhyming lines). Find ways to use the rhymes to advance Hermia's thoughts, but avoid letting them get in the way of the meaning of the sentences.*

WHERE ELSE TO LOOK ☞   *Helena (A Midsummer Night's Dream, p. 34) and Adriana (The Comedy of Errors, p. 26) also feel mistreated.*

Hermia

66 Now I but chide;* but I should use* thee worse,
For thou, I fear, hast given me cause to curse.
If thou hast slain Lysander in his sleep,
Being o'er shoes in blood,* plunge in the deep,
And kill me too.
The sun was not so true unto the day
As he to me: would he have stolen away
From sleeping Hermia? I'll believe as soon
This whole earth may be bor'd, and that the moon
May through the centre creep, and so displease
Her brother's noontide with th'Antipodes.*
It cannot be but thou hast murder'd him:
So should a murderer look; so dead, so grim.
Out, dog! Out, cur! Thou driv'st me past the bounds
Of maiden's patience. Hast thou slain him, then?
Henceforth be never number'd among men!
O, once tell true, tell true, even for my sake!
Durst* thou have look'd upon him being awake,
And hast thou kill'd him sleeping? **99**

(Act 3, scene 2, lines 45–70, with cuts)

GLOSSARY

I but chide – I'm only scolding
use – treat
o'er shoes – foot deep
This whole earth... noontide with th'Antipodes – the moon might slip
   through a hole drilled in the earth, and so baffle the sun by bringing
   darkness to the inhabitants of the other side of the world.
Durst – did you dare

A Midsummer Night's Dream

WHO ☞ *Puck (or Robin Goodfellow), a mischievous spirit.*

WHERE ☞ *The Palace of Duke Theseus in Athens.*

WHO ELSE IS THERE ☞ *Puck is alone.*

WHAT IS HAPPENING ☞ *It is the end of the play. Night has fallen and Puck enters carrying a broom, creating the mood of mystery and fear that darkness brings.*

WHAT TO THINK ABOUT ☞

- *Imagine that you are in the dark, lit only by a candle as you say your words.*

- *See how scary you can be as you talk of graves and ghosts.*

- *Find a way of using the final rhyming couplet (pair of rhyming lines) to bring the speech to a strong close.*

WHERE ELSE TO LOOK ☞ *The Courtesan (The Comedy of Errors, p. 28) also talks directly to the audience.*

Puck

" Now the hungry lion roars,
And the wolf behowls the moon,
Whilst the heavy ploughman snores,
All with weary task fordone.
Now the wasted brands* do glow,
Whilst the screech-owl, screeching loud,
Puts the wretch that lies in woe
In remembrance of a shroud.
Now it is the time of night
That the graves, all gaping wide,
Every one lets forth his sprite*
In the church-way paths to glide;
And we fairies, that do run
By the triple Hecate's team
From the presence of the sun,*
Following darkness like a dream,
Now are frolic.* Not a mouse
Shall disturb this hallow'd house:
I am sent with broom before,
To sweep the dust behind the door. **"**

(Act 5, scene 2, lines 1–20)

GLOSSARY

wasted brands – embers, burnt-out logs
sprite – spirit/ghost
By the triple Hecate's team... sun – alongside the chariot, drawn by
    dragons, of the classical three-crowned goddess of darkness Hecate
    (here pronounced Heck-at) on her flight from the sun
frolic – merry

The Merchant of Venice

WHO ☞ *Portia.*

WHERE ☞ *Portia's home in Belmont, outside Venice.*

WHO ELSE IS THERE ☞ *Bassanio, his friend Gratiano, her maid Nerissa, and others.*

WHAT IS HAPPENING ☞ *A series of young men have come to Belmont to win the young heiress Portia for their wife. As Portia explains to each of them in turn, her father has laid down a strict condition in his will. He has left three caskets – one of gold, one of silver, and one of lead. Bassanio must choose the correct casket – the leaden one, containing Portia's portrait – if he is to marry her; if he chooses the wrong box, he may never marry anyone else. Others have come to win Portia's hand, but all have failed. Bassanio is different – Portia has fallen in love with him. There are two speeches by Portia in this book, both from the same scene. In this first one she instructs the others in the room to stand aside, and tells Bassanio to make his choice.*

WHAT TO THINK ABOUT ☞

- *Portia tells the others what to do, but can then only watch as Bassanio makes his choice. Plan who moves where, and which of her words the others hear.*

- *This is an exciting moment. Portia's heart must be racing. How can you convey this through your voice, breathing and movement?*

- *Picture Bassanio as you speak to him, and everything that Portia finds attractive about him.*

WHERE ELSE TO LOOK ☞ *Juliet (Romeo and Juliet, pp. 80, 82 and 84) is also anxious and in love.*

Portia

66 Away, then! I am lock'd in one of them:
If you do love me, you will find me out.
Nerissa and the rest, stand all aloof.*
Let music sound while he doth make his choice;
Then, if he lose, he makes a swan-like end,*
Fading in music. That the comparison
May stand more proper, my eye shall be the stream
And watery death-bed for him. He may win;
And what is music then? Then music is
Even as the flourish when true subjects bow
To a new-crownèd monarch: such it is,
As are those dulcet* sounds in break of day
That creep into the dreaming bridegroom's ear,
And summon him to marriage. Now he goes
With no less presence, but with much more love,
Than young Alcides,* when he did redeem
The virgin tribute paid by howling Troy
To the sea-monster. I stand for sacrifice;
The rest, aloof, are the Dardanian wives,*
With blearèd visages come forth to view
The issue of the exploit. Go, Hercules!
Live thou, I live: with much, much more dismay
I view the fight than thou that mak'st the fray. 99

(Act 3, scene 2, lines 40–62)

GLOSSARY

aloof – aside
swan-like end – like a dying swan (birds proverbially thought to sing their
    sweetest as they die)
dulcet – sweet
Alcides – (pronounced 'Al-side-ees') Hercules, the Greek superhero who
    saved the virgin Hesione from being sacrificed to a sea-creature by
    the people of Troy who just stood and watched
Dardanian wives – women of Troy

The Merchant of Venice

WHO ☞ *Portia.*

WHERE ☞ *Portia's home in Belmont, outside Venice.*

WHO ELSE IS THERE ☞ *Bassanio, his friend Gratiano, her maid Nerissa, and others.*

WHAT IS HAPPENING ☞ *A series of young men have come to Belmont to win the young heiress Portia for their wife. As Portia explains to each of them in turn, her father has laid down a strict condition in his will. He has left three caskets – one of gold, one of silver, and one of lead. Bassanio must choose the correct casket – the leaden one, containing Portia's portrait – if he is to marry her; if he chooses the wrong box, he may never marry anyone else. Others have come to win Portia's hand, but all have failed. Bassanio is different – Portia has fallen in love with him. There are two speeches by Portia in this book, both from the same scene. In this second, Bassanio has just found her portrait by opening the correct box. She gives herself to Bassanio, together with everything she possesses. As a token of her love, she also gives him a ring which he must never lose.*

WHAT TO THINK ABOUT ☞

- *What are Portia's feelings at finally finding a husband after all the men who have come to win her hand?*

- *How does she want her relationship with Bassanio to proceed?*

- *Where is the ring from, and what significance does it hold for her?*

WHERE ELSE TO LOOK ☞ *Juliet (Romeo and Juliet, pp. 80 and 82) also pledges a commitment to the person she loves.*

Portia

❝ You see me, Lord Bassanio, where I stand,
Such as I am: though for myself alone
I would not be ambitious in my wish
To wish myself much better; yet, for you,
I would be trebled twenty times myself,
A thousand times more fair, ten thousand times more rich,
That only to stand high in your account,
I might in virtue, beauties, livings, friends,
Exceed account; but the full sum of me
Is sum of something – which, to term in gross,*
Is an unlesson'd girl, unschool'd, unpractisèd.
Happy in this, she is not yet so old
But she may learn; happier than this,
She is not bred so dull but she can learn;
Happiest of all is that her gentle spirit
Commits itself to yours to be directed,
As from her lord, her governor, her king.
Myself and what is mine to you and yours
Is now converted. But now* I was the lord
Of this fair mansion, master of my servants,
Queen o'er myself; and even now, but now,
This house, these servants, and this same myself
Are yours, my lord: I give them with this ring;
Which when you part from, lose, or give away,
Let it presage* the ruin of your love
And be my vantage to exclaim on* you. **❞**

(Act 3, scene 2, lines 149–75)

GLOSSARY

term in gross – summarise in general terms
But now – until just now
presage – foretell
vantage to exclaim on – opportunity to denounce

As You Like It

WHO ☞ *Celia, daughter to Duke Frederick.*

WHERE ☞ *The Duke's court.*

WHO ELSE IS THERE ☞ *Rosalind, her cousin.*

WHAT IS HAPPENING ☞ *Duke Frederick has taken control of the court from his brother, Duke Senior, and sent him into exile. He now accuses Duke Senior's daughter Rosalind of plotting treason and says that she too must be banished. His own daughter, Celia, comforts her cousin and says that she will go with her.*

WHAT TO THINK ABOUT ☞

- *What does Celia think of her father's action?*
- *How is she affected by the split loyalties between her father and her cousin?*
- *At what moment does Celia come up with her plan, and what thought-process leads to it?*

WHERE ELSE TO LOOK ☞ *Miranda (The Tempest, p. 20) is also caught between loyalty to her father and to the man she loves.*

Celia

❝ O my poor Rosalind! Whither wilt thou go?
Wilt thou change fathers? I will give thee mine.
I charge* thee, be not thou more griev'd than I am.
Prithee be cheerful. Know'st thou not the Duke
Hath banish'd me, his daughter?
Shall we be sunder'd?* Shall we part, sweet girl?
No; let my father seek another heir.
Therefore devise with me how we may fly,
Whither to go, and what to bear with us;
And do not seek to take your change upon you*
To bear your griefs yourself and leave me out;
For by this heaven, now at our sorrows pale,*
Say what thou canst, I'll go along with thee. **❞**

(Act 1, scene 3 , lines 83–98, with cuts)

GLOSSARY

charge – command, instruct
sunder'd – separated, parted
take your change upon you – assume responsibility for your social
    transformation
this heaven... at our sorrows pale – the sky... darkening towards twilight
    as if in sympathy with our woes

As You Like It

WHO ☞ *Rosalind, disguised as 'Ganymede'.*

WHERE ☞ *The forest of Arden.*

WHO ELSE IS THERE ☞ *Silvius, a shepherd, and Phoebe, a shepherdess.*

WHAT IS HAPPENING ☞ *Banished by the Duke to the forest of Arden, the beautiful Rosalind has disguised herself as a man for protection and called herself Ganymede. She meets the shepherd Silvius and the shepherdess Phoebe. Silvius is in love with Phoebe but she scorns him. Rosalind intervenes to tell Phoebe that she has no right to treat Silvius in such a way, and that she should think herself lucky that Silvius is in love with someone as unattractive as her.*

WHAT TO THINK ABOUT ☞

- *Place Silvius and Phoebe, and come between them, so it is clear who you are talking to.*

- *Some lines may be said more privately to Phoebe than others which Silvius can hear as well.*

- *Play the surprise of realising that Phoebe may be falling in love with Rosalind when she 'tangles' her eyes. Be firm in telling her to 'hope not after it'.*

WHERE ELSE TO LOOK ☞ *Helena (All's Well That Ends Well, pp. 50 and 52) also speaks of the qualities of love.*

Rosalind

❝ And why, I pray you? Who might be your mother,*
That you insult, exult, and all at once,
Over the wretched? What though you have no beauty –
As by my faith, I see no more in you
Than without candle may go dark to bed –*
Must you be therefore proud and pitiless?

Why, what means this? Why do you look on me?
I see no more in you than in the ordinary
Of Nature's sale-work.* 'Od's* my little life,
I think she means to tangle my eyes* too!
No, faith, proud mistress, hope not after it:
'Tis not your inky brows, your black silk hair,
Your bugle* eyeballs, nor your cheek of cream,
That can entame my spirits to your worship.
You foolish shepherd, wherefore do you follow her,
Like foggy south* puffing with wind and rain?
You are a thousand times a properer man
Than she a woman: 'tis such fools as you
That make the world full of ill-favour'd* children.
'Tis not her glass,* but you, that flatters her;
And out of you she sees herself more proper
Than any of her lineaments* can show her.
But, mistress, know yourself: down on your knees,
And thank heaven, fasting,* for a good man's love.
For I must tell you friendly in your ear:
Sell when you can; you are not for all markets.
Cry the man mercy;* love him; take his offer:
Foul is most foul, being foul to be a scoffer.*
So take her to thee, shepherd. Fare you well. **99**

(*Act 3, scene 5, lines 40–68*)

GLOSSARY

Who might be your mother – who do you think you are?
I see no more in you... go dark to bed – there's nothing more to admire in
    your looks than in the dark without a candle
ordinary of Nature's sale-work – commonplace examples of the cheap
    goods Nature displays on her stall   *'Od's* – God save
tangle my eyes – entangle me, ensnare my affections
bugle – bulging
foggy south – the south wind that brings rain and fog
ill-favour'd – ugly   *glass* – mirror
lineaments – features   *fasting* – i.e. in a penitential spirit
Cry... mercy – seek forgiveness from
Foul... a scoffer – ugliness is even more ugly when it turns to scorns

All's Well That Ends Well

WHO ☞ *Helena.*

WHERE ☞ *The house of the Countess of Rossillion.*

WHO ELSE IS THERE ☞ *The Countess of Rossillion.*

WHAT IS HAPPENING ☞ *Helena has been left an orphan by the death of her father, and the Countess of Rossillion has taken her into her home. Helena has fallen in love with the Countess's son Bertram, who does not reciprocate her feelings. Helena has a number of strong speeches in the play, of which two are in this book and another in the companion volume of Shakespeare Monologues for Women. Here she summons up the courage to tell the Countess of her love for her son.*

WHAT TO THINK ABOUT ☞

- *The four words 'I love your son' have a line to themselves. Find ways to use the strength of the four single-syllable words and the silence that follows it.*

- *Helena knows her love to be hopeless and does not want to cause offence to the woman who is caring for her.*

- *The opening of the speech is directly addressed to the Countess. Some of the rest might be more introspective.*

WHERE ELSE TO LOOK ☞ *The love of the Jailer's Daughter (The Two Noble Kinsmen, pp. 98, 100 and 102) is also hopeless.*

Helena

❝ Then I confess,
Here on my knee, before high heaven and you,
That before you, and next unto high heaven,
I love your son.
My friends were poor, but honest; so's my love.
Be not offended; for it hurts not him
That he is lov'd of me: I follow him not

By any token of presumptuous suit;*
Nor would I have him till I do deserve him,
Yet never know how that desert should be.
I know I love in vain, strive against hope;
Yet in this captious and intenible sieve*
I still pour in the waters of my love
And lack not to lose still.* Thus, Indian-like,
Religious in mine error, I adore
The sun that looks upon his worshipper
But knows of him no more.* My dearest madam,
Let not your hate encounter with my love
For loving where you do; but if yourself,
Whose agèd honour cites* a virtuous youth,
Did ever in so true a flame of liking
Wish chastely and love dearly, that your Dian*
Was both herself and love: O, then, give pity
To her whose state is such that cannot choose
But lend and give where she is sure to lose;
That seeks not to find that her search implies,*
But riddle-like* lives sweetly where she dies. 99

(Act 1, scene 3 , lines 199–225)

GLOSSARY

by any token of presumptuous suit – out of any sense of improper love
captious and intenible sieve – large sieve that can hold nothing
lack not to lose still – never run out of more water to pour away
Indian-like... knows of him no more – I revere him as fervently and
    erroneously as an Indian worships the oblivious sun
cites – confirms
Dian – Diana, goddess of chastity
that her search implies – what her pursuit presents as its goal
riddle-like – paradoxically

All's Well That Ends Well

WHO ☞ *Helena.*

WHERE ☞ *The house of the Countess of Rossillion.*

WHO ELSE IS THERE ☞ *The Countess of Rossillion.*

WHAT IS HAPPENING ☞ *Helena has been left an orphan by the death of her father, and the Countess of Rossillion has taken her into her home. Helena has fallen in love with the Countess's son Bertram, who does not reciprocate her feelings. Helena's father was a doctor, and she uses his remedies to cure the King's illness. In thanks the King offers to grant any request she makes of him, and she asks for Bertram's hand in marriage. Bertram reluctantly marries Helena, but immediately goes off to join the army at war in Italy. Helena has a number of strong speeches in the play, of which two are in this book and another in the companion volume of Shakespeare Monologues for Women. Here Helena has just read a letter in which Bertram says that until he no longer has a wife he will not return to France. Helena is stricken with guilt that she might have driven the man she loves off to be killed in battle.*

WHAT TO THINK ABOUT ☞

- *Follow Helena's thought process until she decides that it is better for Bertram to return home, and her to leave.*

- *There is real fear and danger in her thoughts of guns, bullets, and battles.*

- *The final rhyming couplet (pair of rhyming lines) has a strong first line but ends more quietly on the second.*

WHERE ELSE TO LOOK ☞ *Perdita (The Winter's Tale, pp. 54 and 56) and Ophelia (Hamlet, p. 88) are both scared and in love.*

Helena

❝ 'Till I have no wife, I have nothing in France.'
Nothing in France, until he has no wife!

Thou shalt have none, Rossillion, none in France;
Then hast thou all again. Poor lord! Is't I
That chase thee from thy country and expose
Those tender limbs of thine to the event
Of the none-sparing war? and is it I
That drive thee from the sportive court, where thou
Wast shot at with fair eyes, to be the mark*
Of smoky muskets? O you leaden messengers,*
That ride upon the violent speed of fire,
Fly with false aim; move the still-peering air*
That sings with piercing; do not touch my lord.
Whoever shoots at him, I set him there;
Whoever charges on his forward breast,
I am the caitiff* that do hold him to't;
And, though I kill him not, I am the cause
His death was so effected. Better 'twere
I met the ravin* lion when he roar'd
With sharp constraint of hunger; better 'twere
That all the miseries which nature owes
Were mine at once. No, come thou home, Rossillion,
Whence honour but of danger wins a scar,*
As oft it loses all: I will be gone;
My being here it is that holds thee hence:
Shall I stay here to do't? No, no, although
The air of paradise did fan the house
And angels offic'd all:* I will be gone,
That pitiful rumour may report my flight,
To consolate* thine ear. Come, night; end, day!
For with the dark, poor thief, I'll steal away. **99**

(*Act 3, scene 2, lines 102–32*)

GLOSSARY

mark – target   *leaden messengers* – bullets
still-peering air – ever-watchful air
caitiff – coward, worthless person   *ravin* – starving, ravenous
Whence honour but of danger wins a scar – from that dangerous place where the
   best that honourable behaviour can achieve is the survival of a wound
offic'd all – performed all household services   *consolate* – console

The Winter's Tale

WHO ☞ *Perdita.*

WHERE ☞ *A shepherd's cottage in Bohemia.*

WHO ELSE IS THERE ☞ *Florizel, Prince of Bohemia.*

WHAT IS HAPPENING ☞ *Perdita, a young shepherdess, is in truth, but unknown to her, a princess from neighbouring Sicilia, abandoned at birth. She and Florizel, the Prince of Bohemia, have fallen in love. It is the annual sheep-shearing festival and Perdita is dressed as 'Mistress of the Feast', while Florizel is wearing shepherd's clothing. There are two of Perdita's speeches in this book. In this first one she talks to Florizel of the impossibility of their love – he a prince, she a 'poor lowly maid'.*

WHAT TO THINK ABOUT ☞

- *How difficult is it for Perdita to tell Florizel that they cannot be together?*

- *Why is she frightened of the King finding out about their mutual attraction?*

- *How does she rate her status compared to that of her lover?*

WHERE ELSE TO LOOK ☞ *Others caught up in a seemingly impossible love are Juliet (Romeo and Juliet, pp. 80, 82 and 84) and Helena (All's Well That Ends Well, pp. 50 and 52).*

Perdita

“ Sir, my gracious lord,
To chide at your extremes* it not becomes me:
O, pardon, that I name them! Your high self,
The gracious mark o' th' land,* you have obscur'd
With a swain's wearing;* and me, poor lowly maid,
Most goddess-like prank'd up.* But that our feasts
In every mess* have folly, and the feeders
Digest it with a custom, I should blush
To see you so attir'd, sworn, I think,
To show myself a glass.*
To me the difference forges dread; your greatness
Hath not been us'd to fear. Even now I tremble
To think your father, by some accident,
Should pass this way as you did. O, the Fates!
How would he look, to see his work, so noble,
Vilely bound up?* What would he say? Or how
Should I, in these my borrow'd flaunts,* behold
The sternness of his presence? **”**

(*Act 4, scene 4, lines 5–24, with cut*)

GLOSSARY

chide at your extremes – rebuke your hyperbolic description of me
mark o' th' land – object of general attention
a swain's wearing – peasant garments
prank'd up – in fancy dress
mess – group of diners
glass – mirror
Vilely bound up – basely dressed
flaunts – ostentatious clothes

The Winter's Tale

WHO ☞ *Perdita.*

WHERE ☞ *A shepherd's cottage in Bohemia.*

WHO ELSE IS THERE ☞ *Florizel, Prince of Bohemia.*

WHAT IS HAPPENING ☞ *Perdita, a young shepherdess is in truth, but unknown to her, a princess from neighbouring Sicilia, abandoned at birth. She and Florizel, the Prince of Bohemia, have fallen in love. It is the annual sheep-shearing festival and Perdita is dressed as 'Mistress of the Feast', while Florizel is wearing shepherd's clothing. There are two of Perdita's speeches in this book. In this second speech, King Polixenes, Florizel's father, has just found them together. In a rage he threatens to disfigure Perdita and hang the man she thinks to be her father.*

WHAT TO THINK ABOUT ☞

- *Perdita feared that this would happen. What mixture of fear, anger, heartbreak, and other feelings are going through her mind?*

- *What are her feelings towards Florizel?*

- *What does she think will happen next?*

WHERE ELSE TO LOOK ☞ *Others caught up in seemingly impossible love are Juliet (Romeo and Juliet, pp. 80, 82 and 84) and Helena (All's Well That Ends Well, pp. 50 and 52).*

Perdita

❝ Even here undone!
I was not much afeard; for once or twice
I was about to speak and tell him plainly,
The selfsame sun that shines upon his court
Hides not his visage* from our cottage but
Looks on alike. Will't please you, sir, be gone?
I told you what would come of this. Beseech you,
Of your own state take care: this dream of mine
Being now awake, I'll queen it no inch farther,*
But milk my ewes and weep.
How often have I told you 'twould be thus!
How often said, my dignity* would last
But till 'twere known! **❞**

(Act 4, scene 4, lines 441–76, with cuts)

GLOSSARY

visage – face
I'll queen it no inch farther – I won't pretend to royalty for a moment
     longer
dignity – worth (i.e. as a prince's prospective bride)

Pericles

WHO ☞ *Marina.*

WHERE ☞ *A brothel in Mytilene.*

WHO ELSE IS THERE ☞ *Boult, servant to the brothel keeper.*

WHAT IS HAPPENING ☞ *Marina has been captured by pirates, brought to Mytilene, and sold to a brothel. Her beauty and her virginity make her an excellent object for sale, but she resists all of Boult's attempts to persuade her to go with Lysimachus, the man who has bought her services. 'What would you have me do?', he asks her.*

WHAT TO THINK ABOUT ☞

- *The speech falls into three parts: the first her advice to Boult; the second a plea to the gods; and the third the list of alternative services she suggests for the man who has paid for her time. Each has a different tone.*

- *The line to the gods could be played as an aside to the audience, or else as if to the gods themselves.*

- *Decide exactly how to give Boult the money.*

- *The final section might seem to Marina like a sensible idea, or else reflect her desperate attempt to find an escape from her terrible situation.*

WHERE ELSE TO LOOK ☞ *The Courtesan (The Comedy of Errors, p. 28) is more happily pragmatic in her role as a prostitute.*

Marina

❝ Do anything but this thou doest. Empty
Old receptacles, or common shores, of filth;
Serve by indenture* to the common hangman:
Any of these ways are yet better than this.
For what thou professest, a baboon, could he speak,
Would own a name too dear.* O, that the gods
Would safely deliver me from this place!
Here, here's gold for thee.
If that thy master would make gain by me,
Proclaim that I can sing, weave, sew, and dance,
With other virtues which I'll keep from boast;
And I will undertake all these to teach.
I doubt not but this populous city will
Yield many scholars. **❞**

(Act 4, scene 6, lines 170–83)

GLOSSARY

by indenture – as an apprentice
a baboon… name too dear – even a baboon, were he able to speak, would
   profess himself above such grossness

The Histories

King John

WHO ☞ *The First Citizen (of Angiers).*

WHERE ☞ *On the walls of the city of Angiers in Northern France, 1172.*

WHO ELSE IS THERE ☞ *King Philip of France, King John of England, their armies, and others.*

WHAT IS HAPPENING ☞ *Richard I has died. He was King of the Angevin Empire which covered England and much of France. His brother John has inherited the throne but King Philip of France believes that John's nephew Arthur should be the rightful king. War has broken out. At the Battle of Angiers both the French and the English claim victory, but the result is stalemate. The First Citizen of the city suggests that further bloodshed can be avoided if King Philip's eldest son Lewis (the Dauphin) marries King John's niece Blanche and so unite the kingdoms.*

WHAT TO THINK ABOUT ☞

- *The First Citizen makes a clear and logical argument to the warring kings which she believes will lead to peace.*

- *She is talking to two implacable enemies. Where are they and how does she shift focus between them?*

- *How vulnerable does the First Citizen feel her city is, mediating between these two powerful armies?*

WHERE ELSE TO LOOK ☞ *Marina (Pericles, p. 58) and Desdemona (Othello, pp. 92 and 94) also have to plead, though in very different ways, with those whose actions are affecting them badly.*

First Citizen

❝ Hear us, great kings: vouchsafe* awhile to stay,
And I shall show you peace and fair-fac'd league;*
Win you this city without stroke* or wound;

Rescue those breathing lives to die in beds,
That here come sacrifices for the field:
Persèver* not, but hear me, mighty kings.
That daughter there of Spain, the Lady Blanche,
Is niece to England: look upon the years
Of Lewis the Dauphin and that lovely maid.
If lusty love should go in quest of beauty,
Where should he find it fairer than in Blanche?
If zealous love should go in search of virtue,
Where should he find it purer than in Blanche?
If love ambitious sought a match of birth,*
Whose veins bound richer blood than Lady Blanche?
Such as she is, in beauty, virtue, birth,
Is the young Dauphin every way complete:
If not complete of, say he is not she;
And she again wants nothing, to name want,
If want it be not that she is not he.*
This union shall do more than battery* can
To our fast-closèd* gates; for at this match,
With swifter spleen than powder can enforce,*
The mouth of passage shall we fling wide ope,
And give you entrance: but without this match,
The sea enragèd is not half so deaf,*
Lions more confident, mountains and rocks
More free from motion, no, not Death himself
In mortal fury half so peremptory,*
As we to keep this city. **99**

(Act 2, scene 1, lines 439–71, with cuts)

GLOSSARY

vouchsafe – promise   *fair-fac'd league* – an amicable alliance
stroke – the blow of a sword   *Persèver* – continue
match of birth – appropriately aristocratic alliance
If want it be not that she is not he – unless her only fault is not being him
battery – bombardment   *fast-closèd* – tightly shut
at this match… than powder can enforce – on the completion of this
   marriage ('match'), and more keenly and quickly than the ignition of
   gunpowder (with a 'match')
deaf – noisily oblivious   *peremptory* – determined

Henry IV, Part Two

WHO ☞ *Mistress Quickly, hostess of a pub in Eastcheap.*

WHERE ☞ *A street in London.*

WHO ELSE IS THERE ☞ *Fang and Snare, two sergeants.*

WHAT IS HAPPENING ☞ *Sir John Falstaff, a fat old drunk, and his drinking companions have been causing grief to Mistress Quickly. Things have got so bad that she has called on two law officers to have him arrested for the huge debt of 'a hundred mark'.*

WHAT TO THINK ABOUT ☞

- *Mistress Quickly has an odd way with language, often not quite pronouncing her words correctly, and being inadvertently rude.*

- *Find ways of showing Mistress Quickly's anger and frustration in her voice and movements.*

- *Mistress Quickly is a comic character who here shows genuine distress: find a way of negotiating that contradiction.*

WHERE ELSE TO LOOK ☞ *Adriana (The Comedy of Errors, p. 26) also seethes with anger, and the Courtesan (The Comedy of Errors, p. 28) is also after what she is owed.*

Mistress Quickly

❝ Alas the day! Take heed of him: he stabbed me in mine own house, and that most beastly. In good faith, he cares not what mischief he doth if his weapon be out: he will foin* like any devil; he will spare neither man, woman, nor child. I am undone by his going;* I warrant you, he's an infinitive thing upon my score.* Good Master Fang, hold him sure; good Master Snare, let him not 'scape. He comes continuantly* to Pie Corner – saving your manhoods – to buy a saddle; and he is indited to dinner to the Lubber's Head in Lombard Street, to Master Smooth's the silkman.* I pray you, since my exion* is entered, and my case so openly known to the world, let him be brought in to his answer. A hundred mark is a long one for a lone woman to bear; and I have borne, and borne, and borne; and have been fubbed off,* and fubbed off, and fubbed off, from this day to that day, that it is a shame to be thought on. There is no honesty in such dealing, unless a woman should be made an ass, and a beast, to bear every knave's wrong. **❞**

(Act 2, scene 1, from line 15, with cuts)

GLOSSARY

foin – thrust, lunge
undone by his going – ruined by his actions
infinitive… score – infinite, bottomless… bar-tab, credit account
continuantly – at any moment (but also 'incontinently', or 'continually')
silkman – dealer in luxury fabrics
exion – action
fubbed off – put off (as we say 'fobbed off')

Henry VI, Part One

WHO ☞ *Joan la Pucelle.*

WHERE ☞ *War-torn France, 1430.*

WHO ELSE IS THERE ☞ *Joan is alone until joined by the spirits she conjures.*

WHAT IS HAPPENING ☞ *Joan la Pucelle (the Virgin), better known as Joan of Arc, is a young peasant girl who has led the French army in victory against the English. She appears in Henry VI, Part One, and Shakespeare gives her some of the best speeches in the play. Two of them are in this book and another can be found in the companion volume Shakespeare Monologues for Women. Here, near the end of the play, the French have been defeated by the English and a desperate Joan calls on supernatural forces to give her help.*

WHAT TO THINK ABOUT ☞

- *Are the fiends that come real, or might they be figments of Joan's imagination?*

- *Follow the physical and emotional journey of the speech from Joan coming from the battle, to her summoning up the spirits, to her offer of self-sacrifice, and to her eventual exhaustion.*

- *In what ways, with her voice and actions, can Joan try and conjure these spirits? Think of this as a spell.*

WHERE ELSE TO LOOK ☞ *Hecate (Macbeth, p. 86) is a supernatural creature, while Marina (Pericles, p. 58) is in a similarly desperate situation.*

Joan la Pucelle

❝ The regent* conquers, and the Frenchmen fly.
Now help, ye charming spells and periapts;*
And ye, choice spirits that admonish me
And give me signs of future accidents.

[Enter Fiends.]

This speedy and quick appearance argues proof
Of your accustom'd diligence* to me.
Now, ye familiar spirits, that are cull'd
Out of the powerful regions under earth,
Help me this once, that France may get the field.*

[They walk, and speak not.]

O, hold me not with silence over-long!
Where I was wont to feed you with my blood,
I'll lop a member off* and give it you
In earnest of* a further benefit,
So you do* condescend to help me now.

[They shake their heads.]

Cannot my body nor blood-sacrifice
Entreat you to your wonted furtherance?*
Then take my soul, my body, soul and all,
Before that England give the French the foil.*

[They depart.]

See, they forsake me! Now the time is come
That France must vail her lofty-plumèd crest*
And let her head fall into England's lap.
My ancient incantations are too weak,
And hell too strong for me to buckle* with:
Now, France, thy glory droopeth to the dust. 💬

(Act 5, scene 3, lines 1–29, with cuts)

GLOSSARY

regent – ruling viceroy (in fact the English Duke of York)
periapts – written charms   *accustom'd diligence* – usual obedience
get the field – win the battle
lop a member off – cut off one of my own limbs
earnest of – payment for   *So you do* – on condition that you
wonted furtherance – accustomed aid   *the foil* – defeat
vail her lofty-plumèd crest – lower her proudly adorned helmet (in
    homage)
buckle – fight

Henry VI, Part One

WHO ☞ *Joan la Pucelle.*

WHERE ☞ *The camp of the Duke of York, the English Regent, in France, 1431.*

WHO ELSE IS THERE ☞ *The Dukes of York and Warwick, and others.*

WHAT IS HAPPENING ☞ *Joan la Pucelle (the Virgin), better known as Joan of Arc, is a young peasant girl who has led the French army in victory against the English. She appears in Henry VI, Part One, and Shakespeare gives her some of the best speeches in the play. Two of them are in this book and another can be found in the companion volume, Shakespeare Monologues for Women. Here, near the end of the play, in her last appearance, the French have been finally defeated and Joan captured by the English. Joan is about to be burnt at the stake but not before she has told her captors what she thinks of them.*

WHAT TO THINK ABOUT ☞

- *There is an air of regality about Joan, who believes herself to have been chosen by God.*

- *She has nothing but contempt for the English who have captured her.*

- *After being asked to be led to her death, there can be a pause before Joan gives her final curse. How can you best use your voice to give power to that curse?*

WHERE ELSE TO LOOK ☞ *Juliet (Romeo and Juliet, p. 84) and The Jailer's Daughter (The Two Noble Kinsmen, p. 102) each faces death in a different way.*

Joan la Pucelle

❝ First, let me tell you whom you have condemn'd:
Not me begotten of a shepherd swain,*
But issued from the progeny* of kings;
Virtuous and holy, chosen from above,
By inspiration of celestial grace,
To work exceeding miracles on earth.
I never had to do with wicked spirits.
But you, that are polluted with your lusts,
Stain'd with the guiltless blood of innocents,
Corrupt and tainted with a thousand vices,
Because you want the grace that others have,
You judge it straight a thing impossible
To compass wonders* but by help of devils.
No, misconceivèd! Joan of Arc hath been
A virgin from her tender infancy,
Chaste and immaculate in very thought,
Whose maiden blood, thus rigorously effus'd,*
Will cry for vengeance at the gates of heaven.
Then lead me hence, with whom I leave my curse:
May never glorious sun reflex* his beams
Upon the country where you make abode;
But darkness and the gloomy shade of death
Environ you, till mischief and despair
Drive you to break your necks or hang yourselves! **❞**

(Act 5, scene 4, lines 36–91, with cuts)

GLOSSARY

begotten of a shepherd swain – fathered by a peasant shepherd
progeny – descendants, ancestry
compass wonders – achieve miracles
No, misconceivèd! – i.e. such assumptions of yours are so wrong! (The
    line might also be punctuated 'No misconceivèd…' , i.e. not being
    the illegitimate daughter of a peasant…)
rigorously effus'd – copiously shed
reflex – shine

Henry VIII

WHO ☞ *Anne Boleyn.*

WHERE ☞ *The Queen's apartments at the Palace of Westminster (c. 1530).*

WHO ELSE IS THERE ☞ *An old lady.*

WHAT IS HAPPENING ☞ *King Henry VIII is married to Katherine of Aragon, whom he is planning to divorce. Here Anne Boleyn, who will marry Henry and become Queen herself, pities Katherine and tells an old lady that it is better to be born poor than be born a queen and suffer in the way Katherine is suffering.*

WHAT TO THINK ABOUT ☞

- *What does Anne know of love and rejection?*

- *How real is her pity for Katherine?*

- *How strong are her own feelings for Henry?*

- *Would she really not like the riches and glamour that go with royalty?*

WHERE ELSE TO LOOK ☞ *The Princess of France (Love's Labour's Lost, p. 32) and The Jailer's Daughter (The Two Noble Kinsmen, pp. 98 and 100) also talk of the transience of love.*

Anne

❝ Here's the pang that pinches:*
His highness having liv'd so long with her, and she
So good a lady that no tongue could ever
Pronounce dishonour of her – by my life,
She never knew harm-doing – O, now, after
So many courses of the sun enthron'd,*
Still growing in a majesty and pomp the which
To leave a thousand-fold more bitter than
'Tis sweet at first t'acquire,* after this process,
To give her the avaunt,* it is a pity

Would move a monster.

     O, God's will! Much better
She ne'er had known pomp: though't be temporal,
Yet, if that quarrel,* fortune, do divorce
It from the bearer, 'tis a sufferance panging
As soul and body's severing.*

     Verily,
I swear, 'tis better to be lowly born,
And range with humble livers in content,*
Than to be perk'd up in a glistering grief,
And wear a golden sorrow.* 🙶

     (Act 2, scene 3, lines 1–26, with cuts)

GLOSSARY

the pang that pinches – the agonising pain
So many courses of the sun enthron'd – having been Queen for so long (i.e. measured by the circuit of the sun)
To leave a thousand-fold more bitter than / 'Tis sweet at first to acquire – i.e. giving things up is a thousand times more bitter than the sweetness of getting them in the first place.
give her the avaunt – abruptly tell her to get lost (i.e. divorce her)
quarrel – quarreller, turbulent influence
a sufferance panging / As soul and body's severing – as agonising a pain as death itself
range with humble livers in content – be counted among, and share the contentment of, lowlier people
be perk'd up in a glistering grief… wear a golden sorrow – be spruced up and crowned in gorgeous clothes while utterly miserable

The Tragedies

Troilus and Cressida

WHO ☞ *Cressida.*

WHERE ☞ *A street in besieged Troy.*

WHO ELSE IS THERE ☞ *Cressida is alone.*

WHAT IS HAPPENING ☞ *Helen, the most beautiful woman in the world and wife of Menelaus, King of the Greek city of Sparta, has been abducted by Paris and taken to Troy to be his wife. A war has raged for ten years as the Greeks have tried to recapture her. Paris's brother Troilus is in love with Cressida. There are three of Cressida's speeches in this book from different parts of the play. Here, early in the play, Troilus has fallen in love with her, and asked her uncle Pandarus to arrange a rendezvous between them. Pandarus has just promised to deliver to her a 'token' of Troilus's love, leaving Cressida alone to her thoughts.*

WHAT TO THINK ABOUT ☞

- *The first line is to Pandarus as he leaves. Make sure Cressida is alone before she says more.*

- *What does she find so attractive about Troilus?*

- *Why does she hold back from admitting that she likes him?*

- *Find a way to use the rhyming couplets she delivers to round off the train each of her considered thoughts.*

WHERE ELSE TO LOOK ☞ *Juliet (Romeo and Juliet, p. 82) and Helena (All's Well That Ends Well, p. 50) are both wary of admitting their love.*

Cressida

❝ By the same token, you are a bawd.*
Words, vows, gifts, tears, and love's full sacrifice
He offers in another's enterprise;
But more in Troilus thousandfold I see
Than in the glass of Pandar's praise may be;
Yet hold I off. Women are angels, wooing;
Things won are done; joy's soul lies in the doing.
That she belov'd* knows nought that knows not this:
Men prize the thing ungain'd more than it is.
That she was never yet that ever knew
Love got so sweet as when desire did sue.*
Therefore this maxim out of love I teach:
'Achievement is command; ungain'd, beseech.'*
Then, though my heart's content* firm love doth bear,
Nothing of that shall from mine eyes appear. **❞**

(*Act 1, scene 2, lines 281–95*)

GLOSSARY

bawd – brothel keeper
the glass of Pandar's praise – the flattering reflections Pandarus presents
    of him
That she belov'd – any adored woman
That she was never… desire did sue – there never was a woman whose
    experience of love wasn't the sweeter for resisting her lover than
    yielding to him
'Achievement is command; ungain'd, beseech' – i.e. a lover's attitude will
    change from submission to domination at the moment we yield to
    him (which it is better to postpone)
my heart's content – the contents of my heart

Troilus and Cressida

WHO ☞   *Cressida.*

WHERE ☞   *The orchard at Pandarus's house, within the besieged city of Troy.*

WHO ELSE IS THERE ☞   *Troilus and Pandarus.*

WHAT IS HAPPENING ☞   *Helen, the most beautiful woman in the world and wife of Menelaus, King of the Greek city of Sparta, has been abducted by Paris and taken to Troy to be his wife. A war has raged for ten years as the Greeks have tried to recapture her. Paris's brother Troilus is in love with Cressida. Using Cressida's uncle Pandarus as a go-between, Troilus and Cressida have declared their love for each other, and Troilus has vowed that he will be so true to her that his name will be synonymous with fidelity in the years to come. Cressida's reply offers an equal and opposite vow, and is followed by Pandarus leading the lovers off to bed.*

WHAT TO THINK ABOUT ☞

- *How excited is Cressida to know that Troilus loves her?*

- *How difficult was it for her to admit her own love?*

- *What are her feelings at being about to make love with Troilus for the first time?*

- *Does her uncle being there affect her behaviour?*

WHERE ELSE TO LOOK ☞   *Juliet (Romeo and Juliet, p. 82) and Helena (All's Well That Ends Well, p. 50) are both wary of admitting their love.*

Cressida

66 Prophet may you be!
If I be false, or swerve a hair from truth,
When time is old and hath forgot itself,
When waterdrops have worn the stones of Troy,
And blind oblivion swallow'd cities up,
And mighty states characterless are grated*
To dusty nothing, yet let memory,
From false to false,* among false maids in love,
Upbraid my falsehood!* When they've said 'As false
As air, as water, wind, or sandy earth,
As fox to lamb, as wolf to heifer's calf,
Pard to the hind,* or stepdame* to her son',
'Yea,' let them say, to stick the heart of* falsehood,
'As false as Cressid.' **99**

(Act 3, scene 2, lines 182–94)

GLOSSARY

characterless are grated – are pulverised without a trace
From false to false – i.e. as the common currency among unfaithful or
    untrustworthy people
Upbraid my falsehood – i.e. castigate my own treacherous infidelity as
    worst of all
Pard... hind – leopard... deer
stepdame – stepmother (often wicked in fairy tales)
stick the heart of – get to the root of, fully summarise, 'nail'

Troilus and Cressida

WHO ☞   *Cressida.*

WHERE ☞   *Pandarus's house in the besieged city of Troy.*

WHO ELSE IS THERE ☞   *Her uncle Pandarus.*

WHAT IS HAPPENING ☞   *Helen, the most beautiful woman in the world and wife of Menelaus, King of the Greek city of Sparta, has been abducted by Paris and taken to Troy to be his wife. A war has raged for ten years as the Greeks have tried to recapture her. Paris's brother Troilus is in love with Cressida, and using Cressida's uncle Pandarus as a go-between, the couple have consummated their love. The third of Cressida's speeches in this book is taken from towards the end of the play. Following the terms of a negotiated agreement, the Trojans will give Cressida to the Greek leader Diomedes in exchange for the captured Trojan leader Antenor. Cressida is still reeling from the news, and her uncle Pandarus has just told her to 'be moderate' – to calm down.*

WHAT TO THINK ABOUT ☞

- *What mixture of emotions must Cressida be feeling?*

- *Does Cressida cry? If so, how difficult is it for her to express her anger through her tears?*

- *How can the rhyming couplet (pair of rhyming lines) at the end of the speech be used to bring it to a conclusion?*

WHERE ELSE TO LOOK ☞   *Other heartbroken lovers include Juliet (Romeo and Juliet, p. 84) and Helena (All's Well That Ends Well, p. 52).*

Cressida

❝ Why tell you me of moderation?
The grief is fine,* full, perfect, that I taste,
And violenteth in a sense as strong*
As that which causeth it: how can I moderate it?
If I could temporise with my affection,
Or brew it to a weak and colder palate,
The like allayment* could I give my grief.
My love admits no qualifying dross;*
No more my grief, in such a precious loss. **❞**

(Act 4, scene 4, lines 2–10)

GLOSSARY

fine – pure, refined, distilled
violenteth in a sense as strong as – seethes in turbulent proportion to
temporise... affection... brew... allayment – compromise with...
    passions... dilute... moderation
qualifying dross – contaminating impurity

Romeo and Juliet

WHO ☞ *Juliet, daughter of Lord and Lady Capulet.*

WHERE ☞ *The balcony of her bedroom, overlooking the garden, in Verona.*

WHO ELSE IS THERE ☞ *Romeo, son of Lord and Lady Montague, with whom she has just fallen in love.*

WHAT IS HAPPENING ☞ *The Montague and Capulet families have been feuding for so long that no one remembers why. Romeo with his friends has just gatecrashed a party at the Capulets' house where he has met Juliet. Romeo and Juliet have fallen in love. There are three speeches by Juliet in this book, and a further two in the companion volume of Shakespeare Monologues for Women. In this first one, Juliet is talking to Romeo, having just realised that he is a Montague. She knows that their parents will never agree to their seeing each other.*

WHAT TO THINK ABOUT ☞

- *How dangerous is their relationship?*

- *What is it about Romeo that Juliet finds so attractive? Picture him as you talk to him.*

- *It is night. How can you create the atmosphere of a secret meeting with your voice and movements?*

WHERE ELSE TO LOOK ☞ *Other girls in love include Portia (The Merchant of Venice, pp. 42 and 44) and Cressida (Troilus and Cressida, pp. 74, 76 and 78).*

Juliet

❝ O Romeo, Romeo, wherefore art thou Romeo?*
Deny thy father and refuse thy name;
Or, if thou wilt not, be but sworn my love,
And I'll no longer be a Capulet.
'Tis but thy name that is my enemy;
Thou art thyself, though not a Montague.
What's Montague? It is nor hand, nor foot,
Nor arm, nor face, nor any other part
Belonging to a man. O, be some other name!
What's in a name? That which we call a rose
By any other name would smell as sweet;
So Romeo would, were he not Romeo call'd,
Retain that dear perfection which he owes*
Without that title. Romeo, doff* thy name,
And for thy name, which is no part of thee,
Take all myself. **❞**

(*Act 2, scene 2, lines 33–49, with cut*)

GLOSSARY

wherefore art thou Romeo? – why must you be (of all people) Romeo?
owes – possesses, owns
doff – take off

Romeo and Juliet

WHO ☞ *Juliet, daughter of Lord and Lady Capulet.*

WHERE ☞ *The balcony of her bedroom, overlooking the garden, in Verona.*

WHO ELSE IS THERE ☞ *Romeo, son of Lord and Lady Montague, with whom she has just fallen in love.*

WHAT IS HAPPENING ☞ *The Montague and Capulet families have been feuding for so long that no one remembers why. Romeo with his friends has just gatecrashed a party at the Capulets' house where he has met Juliet. Romeo and Juliet have fallen in love. There are three speeches by Juliet in this book, and a further two in the companion volume of Shakespeare Monologues for Women. In this second speech, Juliet is embarrassed that Romeo has overheard her talking to herself about her love for him. She is also not sure she can believe him if he says that he loves her.*

WHAT TO THINK ABOUT ☞

- *Juliet does not want her parents, or anyone in the house, to hear her talking to Romeo.*

- *Why does Juliet not trust Romeo to be honest? Has she had boyfriends before?*

- *Why is Juliet embarrassed to have confessed her love?*

WHERE ELSE TO LOOK ☞ *Miranda (The Tempest, p. 20), Portia (The Merchant of Venice, pp. 42 and 44) and Cressida (Troilus and Cressida, pp. 74, 76 and 78) all admit their love.*

Juliet

❝ Thou know'st the mask of night is on my face;
Else would a maiden blush bepaint* my cheek
For that which thou hast heard me speak tonight.
Fain* would I dwell on form – fain, fain deny
What I have spoke; but farewell, compliment!*
Dost thou love me? I know thou wilt say 'Ay',
And I will take thy word. Yet, if thou swear'st,
Thou mayst prove false. At lovers' perjuries*
They say Jove* laughs. O gentle Romeo,
If thou dost love, pronounce it faithfully.
Or if thou thinkest I am too quickly won,
I'll frown, and be perverse, and say thee nay,
So thou wilt woo;* but else, not for the world.
In truth, fair Montague, I am too fond,*
And therefore thou mayst think my behaviour light;
But trust me, gentleman, I'll prove more true
Than those that have more cunning to be strange.*
I should have been more strange, I must confess,
But that thou overheard'st, ere I was ware,*
My true-love passion. Therefore pardon me,
And not impute* this yielding to light love,
Which the dark night hath so discoverèd. **❞**

(*Act 2, scene 2, lines 85–106*)

GLOSSARY

bepaint – colour
Fain – gladly
form… compliment – decorum… formal etiquette
perjuries – lies told under a sworn oath
Jove – Jupiter, the sexually energetic king of the gods
So thou wilt woo – as long as you continue to woo me
fond – madly in love
strange – decorously reserved, aloof
ere I was ware – before I was aware (of your presence)
not impute – do not ascribe

Romeo and Juliet

WHO ☞ *Juliet, daughter of Lord and Lady Capulet.*

WHERE ☞ *Juliet's bedroom, on the eve of her forced marriage.*

WHO ELSE IS THERE ☞ *Juliet is alone.*

WHAT IS HAPPENING ☞ *The Montague and Capulet families have been feuding for so long that no one remembers why. Romeo, a Montague, and Juliet, a Capulet, have fallen in love and married. There are three speeches by Juliet in this book and a further two in the companion volume of Shakespeare Monologues for Women. In this final speech, everything has gone horribly wrong. Romeo has killed Juliet's cousin Tybalt in a fight and been banished. The Friar who married the couple has come up with a plan. To avoid a forced marriage arranged by her parents, Juliet is to take a drug which will induce a temporary coma to make her appear dead. Meanwhile the Friar will get word to Romeo. After saying goodnight to her mother and her nurse, Juliet now prepares herself to drink the drug.*

WHAT TO THINK ABOUT ☞

- *Feel the coldness, emptiness, and darkness of the tomb you will be taken to.*

- *Imagine the bones close by, and the body of your dead cousin next to you, should you wake too soon.*

- *Think about how to hold (and where to put) the vial of drugs.*

- *How brave must Juliet be to drink the drug the Friar has given her?*

- *What is it that finally makes her drink the potion?*

WHERE ELSE TO LOOK ☞ *The Jailer's Daughter (The Two Noble Kinsmen, pp. 98, 100 and 102) is also in love, afraid, and in the dark.*

Juliet

" I have a faint cold fear thrills through my veins,
That almost freezes up the heat of life.
Come, vial.*
What if this mixture do not work at all?
Shall I be married then tomorrow morning?
No, no: this shall forbid it.
How if, when I am laid into the tomb,
I wake before the time that Romeo
Come to redeem me? There's a fearful point!
Or, if I live, is it not very like,
The horrible conceit* of death and night,
Together with the terror of the place –
As in a vault, an ancient receptacle,
Where for these many hundred years the bones
Of all my buried ancestors are pack'd;
Where bloody Tybalt, yet but green in earth,
Lies festering in his shroud; where, as they say,
At some hours in the night spirits resort –
Alack, alack, is it not like that I,
So early waking, what with loathsome smells,
And shrieks like mandrakes* torn out of the earth,
That living mortals, hearing them, run mad –
O, if I wake, shall I not be distraught,
Environèd with* all these hideous fears?
And madly play with my forefathers' joints?*
And pluck the mangled Tybalt from his shroud?
And, in this rage, with some great kinsman's bone,
As with a club, dash out my desperate brains?
O, look! Methinks I see my cousin's ghost
Seeking out Romeo, that did spit his body
Upon a rapier's point. Stay, Tybalt, stay!
Romeo, I come! This do I drink to thee. **"**

(Act 4, scene 3, lines 15–59, with cuts)

GLOSSARY

vial – glass bottle   *conceit* – idea, thought
mandrakes – plant roots that were believed to scream when pulled from
    the ground
Environèd with – surrounded by   *joints* – bones

Macbeth

WHO ☞   *Hecate, goddess of darkness.*

WHERE ☞   *A heath.*

WHO ELSE IS THERE ☞   *Three witches.*

WHAT IS HAPPENING ☞   *The three witches have previously met Macbeth and foretold his future. They are joined one thunderous night by Hecate, goddess of darkness. One of the witches has just asked Hecate why she is so angry.*

WHAT TO THINK ABOUT ☞

- *There are many ways to play such a powerful and supernatural creature. Play with possibilities and choose which works best for you.*

- *Hecate is a goddess amongst witches and her status will affect the way she talks to the other witches.*

- *The speech is written in rhyming couplets (pairs of rhyming lines). Find ways of speaking those rhymes. It might have the feel of a spell about it.*

WHERE ELSE TO LOOK ☞   *Ariel (The Tempest, p. 22) is a very different supernatural creature.*

Hecate

❝ Have I not reason, beldams* as you are,
Saucy* and overbold? How did you dare
To trade and traffic with Macbeth
In riddles and affairs of death;
And I, the mistress of your charms,
The close contriver* of all harms,
Was never call'd to bear my part
Or show the glory of our art?
And, which is worse, all you have done
Hath been but for a wayward* son,

Spiteful and wrathful, who, as others do,
Loves for his own ends, not for you.
But make amends now: get you gone,
And at the pit of Acheron*
Meet me i' th' morning: thither he
Will come to know his destiny.
Your vessels and your spells provide,
Your charms and everything beside.
I am for th'air;* this night I'll spend
Unto a dismal and a fatal end:*
Great business must be wrought ere noon.
Upon the corner of the moon
There hangs a vaporous drop profound;*
I'll catch it ere it come to ground:
And that distill'd by magic sleights*
Shall raise such artificial sprites
As by the strength of their illusion
Shall draw him on to his confusion.
He shall spurn fate, scorn death, and bear
His hopes 'bove wisdom, grace, and fear:
And you all know, security*
Is mortals' chiefest enemy. 🗕🗕

(*Act 3, scene 5, lines 2–33*)

GLOSSARY

beldams – hags
Saucy – rude
charms… close contriver – spells… secret plotter
wayward – disobedient, perverse
Acheron – a river in the Underworld, or Hell
for th'air – about to fly away
dismal… fatal end – disastrous… destined purpose
vaporous drop profound – powerful magic potion
sleights – tricks
security – overconfidence, complacent safety

Hamlet

WHO ☞ *Ophelia.*

WHERE ☞ *A room in her father's house in the castle of Elsinore.*

WHO ELSE IS THERE ☞ *Polonius, her father.*

WHAT IS HAPPENING ☞ *Ophelia is in love with Hamlet, Prince of Denmark. She comes to her father, distressed at Hamlet's behaviour towards her.*

WHAT TO THINK ABOUT ☞

- *Decide if what Ophelia is describing has just happened to her. How fresh is her fear?*

- *Picture each moment of what has happened as Ophelia describes it.*

- *What kind of relationship does Ophelia have with her father, and how easy is it for her to tell him all of this?*

- *Find the backstory of the scene, deciding when Ophelia fell in love with Hamlet and how much he is in love with her. Have there been other scary events in their relationship, or is this the first?*

WHERE ELSE TO LOOK ☞ *Helena (All's Well That Ends Well, pp. 50 and 52) is also distressed at her love.*

Ophelia

❝ O my lord, my lord, I have been so affrighted!
My lord, as I was sewing in my closet,
Lord Hamlet, with his doublet all unbrac'd,*
No hat upon his head, his stockings foul'd,
Ungarter'd, and down-gyvèd* to his ankle;
Pale as his shirt, his knees knocking each other,
And with a look so piteous in purport*
As if he had been loosèd out of hell
To speak of horrors – he comes before me.
He took me by the wrist and held me hard;
Then goes he to the length of all his arm,
And, with his other hand thus o'er his brow,
He falls to such perusal of my face
As he would draw it. Long stay'd he so.
At last, a little shaking of mine arm,
And thrice his head thus waving up and down,
He rais'd a sigh so piteous and profound
As it did seem to shatter all his bulk
And end his being. That done, he lets me go,
And with his head over his shoulder turn'd
He seem'd to find his way without his eyes,
For out o' doors he went without their help,
And to the last bended their light on me. **❞**

(Act 2, scene 1, lines 87–114, with cuts)

GLOSSARY

doublet all unbrac'd – jacket completely unbuttoned
foul'd… Ungarter'd… down-gyvèd – unwashed… unsupported…
    hanging down (like fetters) about the feet (i.e. Prince Hamlet has
    thoroughly – and shockingly – neglected his appearance)
purport – appearance, implications

King Lear

WHO ☞ *Cordelia.*

WHERE ☞ *The camp of the French army, near Dover.*

WHO ELSE IS THERE ☞ *A doctor and soldiers.*

WHAT IS HAPPENING ☞ *King Lear of England has abdicated, intending to divide his kingdom among his three daughters. But believing that Cordelia, his youngest daughter, does not love him sufficiently, he has given no portion to her. In the chaos and fighting that has ensued, Lear has descended into madness. Cordelia has just met her estranged father and here reports to a doctor what she has seen, then sends soldiers to find him.*

WHAT TO THINK ABOUT ☞

- *Although there is a doctor in the scene, it is possible to play the speech as if no one else were there except the soldiers that she sends in search of her father.*

- *How distressing is it to see your father mad and confused?*

- *How strong is her love of Lear, despite all that has happened?*

- *Cordelia has married the King of France and is in England with the French army. How does she deal with her guilt about this?*

WHERE ELSE TO LOOK ☞ *Desdemona (Othello, pp. 92 and 94) has also offended her father.*

Cordelia

❝ Alack, 'tis he: why, he was met even now
As mad as the vex'd sea; singing aloud;
Crown'd with rank fumiter and furrow-weeds,
With bur-docks, hemlock, nettles, cuckoo-flowers,
Darnel, and all the idle weeds that grow
In our sustaining corn.* A century* send forth;
Search every acre in the high-grown field,
And bring him to our eye.
                 All blest secrets,
All you unpublish'd virtues of the earth,*
Spring with my tears! Be aidant and remediate*
In the good man's distress! Seek, seek for him,
Lest his ungovern'd rage dissolve the life
That wants the means to lead it.
                 O dear father,
It is thy business that I go about;
Therefore great France*
My mourning and important* tears hath pitied.
No blown* ambition doth our arms incite,
But love, dear love, and our aged father's right:
Soon may I hear and see him! **❞**

(*Act 4, scene 3, lines 1–29, with cuts*)

GLOSSARY

sustaining corn – nutritious crops (as opposed to the types of weeds previously listed)
century – army unit of a hundred men
unpublish'd virtues of the earth – secret remedies of nature
Be aidant and remediate – supply aid and cure
important – beseeching, importunate
France – i.e. her husband, the King of France (who has pitied her sorrow)
blown – proudly inflated; corruptly swollen

Othello

WHO ☞ *Desdemona.*

WHERE ☞ *The council chamber in Venice.*

WHO ELSE IS THERE ☞ *Brabantio (Desdemona's father), Othello (her new husband), the Duke of Venice, and others.*

WHAT IS HAPPENING ☞ *Desdemona, daughter of the wealthy Venetian citizen Brabantio, has married Othello, a black Army general, against her father's wishes. Brabantio has accused Othello of bewitching his daughter with magic and drugs. He has come to ask the Duke to intervene. There are two speeches by Desdemona in this book, both from the same scene. (They could be joined together to make a longer piece.) For most of this long scene Desdemona has remained silent as all the men talk about and around her. In this first speech, Desdemona talks of her divided loyalty to her father and to her husband.*

WHAT TO THINK ABOUT ☞

• *Where are her father, her husband, and the Duke standing? How does she move between them?*

• *How difficult is it for Desdemona to stand up to her father?*

• *Why does she refer to Othello as 'the Moor my lord'?*

WHERE ELSE TO LOOK ☞ *Also standing up to other adults are Marina (Pericles, p. 56) and Joan la Pucelle (Henry VI, Part One, p. 68).*

Desdemona

66 My noble father,
I do perceive here a divided duty:
To you I am bound for life and education;
My life and education both do learn* me
How to respect you: you are the lord of duty,*
I am hitherto your daughter. But here's my husband,
And so much duty as my mother show'd
To you, preferring you before her father,
So much I challenge that I may profess*
Due to the Moor my lord. **99**

(*Act 1, scene 3, lines 201–10*)

GLOSSARY

learn – teach, instruct
the lord of duty – master of all obedience
challenge that I may profess – claim that which I may equally assert

Othello

WHO ☞ *Desdemona.*

WHERE ☞ *The council chamber in Venice.*

WHO ELSE IS THERE ☞ *Brabantio (Desdemona's father), Othello (her new husband), the Duke of Venice, and others.*

WHAT IS HAPPENING ☞ *Desdemona, daughter of the wealthy Ventian citizen Brabantio, has married Othello, a black Army general, against her father's wishes. Brabantio has accused Othello of bewitching his daughter with magic and drugs. He has come to ask the Duke to intervene. There are two speeches by Desdemona in this book, both from the same scene. (They could be joined together to make a longer piece.) For most of this long scene Desdemona has remained silent as all the men talk about and around her. In this second speech, Desdemona asks the Duke to allow her to accompany Othello on his next military campaign and live with him as his wife.*

WHAT TO THINK ABOUT ☞

- *Why does Desdemona want to go with Othello?*

- *What does she love about him?*

- *Is she being brave in addressing the Duke directly?*

- *What are the 'rites' that she expects, now she and Othello are married?*

WHERE ELSE TO LOOK ☞ *Also standing up to other adults are Marina (Pericles, p. 56) and Joan la Pucelle (Henry VI, Part One, p. 68).*

Desdemona

❝ That I did love the Moor to live with him,
My downright violence and storm of fortunes
May trumpet to the world. My heart's subdued
Even to the very quality of my lord:
I saw Othello's visage* in his mind,
And to his honour and his valiant parts
Did I my soul and fortunes consecrate.
So that, dear lords, if I be left behind,
A moth of peace,* and he go to the war,
The rites for which I love him are bereft me,
And I a heavy interim shall support*
By his dear absence. Let me go with him. **❞**

(Act 1, scene 3, lines 266–77)

GLOSSARY

visage – face
a moth of peace – an idle gadfly
a heavy interim shall support – must endure the grievous anxiety (of
    waiting for his return)

Cymbeline

WHO ☞　*Imogen, daughter of Cymbeline, King of Britain.*

WHERE ☞　*The royal palace in Britain in ancient times.*

WHO ELSE IS THERE ☞　*Pisanio, a servant of her husband Posthumus.*

WHAT IS HAPPENING ☞　*Posthumus has been duped into believing that his wife Imogen has been unfaithful. He writes a letter to his servant Pisanio ordering him to kill her. Pisanio knows Imogen to be innocent and has just revealed the letter to her. She becomes desperate to travel to Milford Haven in Wales to find Posthumus.*

WHAT TO THINK ABOUT ☞

- *How desperate and lonely must Imogen feel?*

- *Has she any idea where Milford Haven is? Or even where Wales is?*

- *Imogen speaks in short, broken phrases. What does this indicate about the way her mind is working and the way she is breathing?*

WHERE ELSE TO LOOK ☞　*Others desperate in their love are Helena (All's Well That Ends Well, pp. 50 and 52) and the Jailer's Daughter (The Two Noble Kinsmen, pp. 98, 100 and 102).*

Imogen

❝ O, for a horse with wings! Hear'st thou, Pisanio?
He is at Milford Haven: read, and tell me
How far 'tis thither. If one of mean affairs*
May plod it in a week, why may not I
Glide thither in a day? Then, true Pisanio,
Who long'st, like me, to see thy lord; who long'st –
O let me bate* – but not like me – yet long'st
But in a fainter kind: O, not like me,
For mine's beyond beyond; say, and speak thick –*
Love's counsellor should fill the bores of hearing,
To th' smothering of the sense* – how far it is
To this same blessèd Milford. And by the way*
Tell me how Wales was made so happy as
T'inherit such a haven: but first of all,
How we may steal from hence, and for the gap
That we shall make in time from our hence-going
And our return, to excuse: but first, how get hence:
Why should excuse be born or ere begot?*
We'll talk of that hereafter. Prithee, speak,
How many score of miles may we well ride
'Twixt hour and hour? **❞**

(Act 3, scene 2, lines 45–65)

GLOSSARY

of mean affairs – concerned with humdrum matters
let me bate – allow me to qualify that statement
speak thick – say lots of things
fill the bores of hearing, / To th' smothering of the sense – fill my ears to
  stop my thoughts
by the way – as we travel
Why should excuse be born or ere begot? – how can any excuse for the time
  it takes us to travel be conceived before ('or ere') we have even begun
  the journey?

The Two Noble Kinsmen

WHO ☞   *The Jailer's Daughter.*

WHERE ☞   *Her father's prison in Athens.*

WHO ELSE IS THERE ☞   *The Jailer's Daughter is alone.*

WHAT IS HAPPENING ☞   *The Jailer's Daughter (we never learn her name) has fallen in love with Palamon, a knight kept captive in her father's prison, and aids his escape. The Jailer's Daughter has four monologues in the play, three of which are included in this book. (The other is in the companion volume of Shakespeare Monologues for Women.) In the first of these, she has just helped the man she loves to escape from jail.*

WHAT TO THINK ABOUT ☞

- *Follow the Jailer's Daughter's train of thought, from her joy at Palamon's escape to her growing doubts as she thinks back over his behaviour.*

- *Why does she love Palamon, and what has she risked for him?*

- *How strong is her conviction that Palamon does, or will, love her?*

- *What does she feel for her father and how is she caught between her loyalty to him and her love of Palamon?*

- *The Jailer's Daughter has fallen madly in love with Palamon, and later in fact goes mad: to what extent does this speech begin this process?*

WHERE ELSE TO LOOK ☞   *Both Juliet (Romeo and Juliet, p. 80) and Desdemona (Othello, p. 92 and 94) are caught by their conflicting loyalty to their parent and lover.*

The Jailer's Daughter

❝ Let all the dukes, and all the devils roar:
He is at liberty! I have ventur'd for him,
And out I have brought him; to a little wood

A mile hence I have sent him, where a cedar,
Higher than all the rest, spreads like a plane
Fast by a brook, and there he shall keep close*
Till I provide him files and food, for yet
His iron bracelets* are not off. O Love,
What a stout-hearted child thou art! My father
Durst better have endur'd cold iron than done it.*
I love him beyond love and beyond reason,
Or wit, or safety; I have made him know it.
I care not, I am desperate. If the law
Find me, and then condemn me for't, some wenches,
Some honest-hearted maids, will sing my dirge
And tell to memory my death was noble,
Dying almost a martyr. That way he takes,
I purpose is my way too. Sure he cannot
Be so unmanly as to leave me here.
If he do, maids will not so easily
Trust men again. And yet he has not thank'd me
For what I have done – no, not so much as kiss'd me,
And that methinks is not so well; nor scarcely
Could I persuade him to become a free man,
He made such scruples of the wrong he did
To me, and to my father.
                 I'll presently
Provide him necessaries,* and pack my clothes up,
And where there is a patch of ground I'll venture,*
So he be with me. By him, like a shadow,
I'll ever dwell. Within this hour the hubbub
Will be all o'er the prison: I am then
Kissing the man they look for. Farewell, Father!
Get many more such prisoners, and such daughters,
And shortly you may keep yourself.* Now to him! 🙶

(Act 2, scene 6, lines 1–39, with cut)

GLOSSARY

keep close – hide   *bracelets* – handcuffs
Durst better have endur'd cold iron than done it – would rather have risked
    imprisonment himself than done this
presently… necessaries – straight away… the means for escape
venture – dare (to join him)   *keep yourself* – have only yourself to guard

The Two Noble Kinsmen

WHO ☞   *The Jailer's Daughter.*

WHERE ☞   *The forest outside Athens.*

WHO ELSE IS THERE ☞   *The Jailer's Daughter is alone.*

WHAT IS HAPPENING ☞   *The Jailer's Daughter (we never learn her name) has fallen in love with Palamon, a knight kept captive in her father's prison, and aids his escape. The Jailer's Daughter has four monologues in the play of which three are in this book. (The other is in the companion volume of Shakespeare Monologues for Women.) Having helped Palamon escape, she has gone to meet him in the forest. Unable to find him, in this second speech she begins to fear what might happen.*

WHAT TO THINK ABOUT ☞

- *Feel how frightening it is to be alone in the forest at night.*

- *Follow the Jailer's Daughter's thoughts and emotions, from fear for herself, to worry for Palamon, thoughts of her father being hanged for what she has done, to contemplating suicide.*

- *Allow the sounds of wolves, crickets, and screech owls to interrupt the speech.*

WHERE ELSE TO LOOK ☞   *Caught between loyalty to parent and lover in different ways are Juliet (Romeo and Juliet, p. 80) and Desdemona (Othello, pp. 92 and 94).*

The Jailer's Daughter

❝ He has mistook the brake* I meant, is gone
After his fancy. 'Tis now well nigh morning.
No matter: would it were perpetual night,
And darkness lord o' th' world. Hark! 'Tis a wolf!
In me hath grief slain fear, and but for one thing
I care for nothing, and that's Palamon.
I reck not if the wolves would jaw me, so
He had this file.* What if I hallooed for him?

I cannot halloo. If I whoop'd, what then?
If he not answer'd, I should call a wolf,
And do him but that service. I have heard
Strange howls this live-long night: why may't not be
They have made prey of him?
                              I'll set it down
He's torn to pieces; they howl'd many together
And then they fed on him. So much for that,
Be bold to ring the bell.* How stand I then?
All's char'd* when he is gone. No, no, I lie,
My father's to be hang'd for his escape,
Myself to beg, if I priz'd life so much
As to deny my act; but that I would not,
Should I try death by dozens.* I am mop'd,*
Food took I none these two days,
Sipp'd some water. I have not clos'd mine eyes
Save when my lids scour'd off their brine.* Alas,
Dissolve my life, let not my sense unsettle,
Lest I should drown, or stab, or hang myself.
O state of nature, fail together in me,
Since thy best props are warp'd! So, which way now?
The best way is the next* way to a grave:
Each errant step beside is torment. Lo,
The moon is down, the crickets chirp, the screech owl
Calls in the dawn. All offices are done
Save what I fail in. But the point is this:
An end, and that is all. **99**

(Act 3, scene 2, lines 1–38, with cut)

GLOSSARY

mistook the brake – misunderstood the thicket
I reck not if… had this file – I don't care if the wolves eat me as long as he
    gets this file
Be bold to ring the bell – toll his death knell vigorously
All's char'd – everything is accomplished (i.e. there's nothing else for me
    to do)
try death by dozens – die dozens of times over
moped – bewildered
I have not closed… scour'd off their brine – I've only closed my eyes to
    push away the tears
next – nearest

The Two Noble Kinsmen

WHO ☞ *The Jailer's Daughter.*

WHERE ☞ *The forest outside Athens.*

WHO ELSE IS THERE ☞ *The Jailer's Daughter is alone.*

WHAT IS HAPPENING ☞ *The Jailer's Daughter (we never learn her name) has fallen in love with Palamon, a knight kept captive in her father's prison, and aids his escape. The Jailer's Daughter has four monologues in the play, of which three are in this book. (The other is in the companion volume of Shakespeare Monologues for Women.) In this third speech, alone, cold, made mad by her unrequited love of Palamon, and believing him dead, the Jailer's Daughter sees a ship sinking at sea. She wishes she could find a frog who will bring her news, and says that she will make a boat out of a seashell and sail to the King of the Pigmies. Her last thought is of her father, about to be hanged for what she has done.*

WHAT TO THINK ABOUT ☞

- *Feel how cold and hungry the Jailer's Daughter is.*

- *Does she really see a ship being wrecked or does she just imagine it?*

- *How does her madness affect her movements and speech?*

- *What does she mean at the end when she says, 'I'll say never a word'? Could she be referring to Palamon or her father?*

WHERE ELSE TO LOOK ☞ *Helena (All's Well That Ends Well, p. 50 and 52) is also desperate in her love.*

The Jailer's Daughter

❝ I am very cold, and all the stars are out too,
The little stars, and all, that look like aglets.*
The sun has seen my folly. Palamon!
Alas no, he's in heaven. Where am I now?
Yonder's the sea, and there's a ship; how't tumbles!
And there's a rock lies watching under water;
Now, now, it beats upon it; now, now, now,
There's a leak sprung, a sound* one; how they cry!
Spoon* her before the wind, you'll lose all else!
Up with a course or two, and tack about, boys.
Goodnight, goodnight, y'are gone. I am very hungry.
Would I could find a fine frog; he would tell me
News from all parts o' th' world, then would I make
A carrack* of a cockleshell, and sail
By east and north-east to the King of Pigmies,
For he tells fortunes rarely.* Now my father,
Twenty to one, is truss'd up in a trice*
Tomorrow morning; I'll say never a word. **❞**

(Act 3, scene 4, lines 1–18)

GLOSSARY

aglets – jewels, spangles
sound – big
Spoon – sail
carrack – galleon
rarely – splendidly
is truss'd up in a trice – hanged in an instant

www.nickhernbooks.co.uk

 facebook.com/nickhernbooks

 twitter.com/nickhernbooks